Negotiating

Patrick Forsyth

- Fast track route to understanding and deploying a key personal communications skill that affects success in both job and career

- Includes powerful methods, concepts and techniques that promote confident negotiations and successful outcomes

- Tips and techniques from gurus such as Chester Karras and detailed verbatim examples of actual negotiations

- Includes a glossary of key concepts and a comprehensive resources guide.

LEADING

08.05

essential management thinking at your fingertips

The right of Patrick Forsyth to be identified as the author of this work has been asserted in accordance with the Copyright, Designs and Patents Act 1988

First published 2002 by
Capstone Publishing (a Wiley company)
8 Newtec Place
Magdalen Road
Oxford OX4 1RE
United Kingdom
http://www.capstoneideas.com

CIP catalogue records for this book are available from the British Library and the US Library of Congress

ISBN 1-84112-361-7

This book is printed on acid-free paper

Substantial discounts on bulk quantities of Capstone books are available to corporations, professional associations and other organizations. Please contact Capstone for more details on +44 (0)1865 798 623 or (fax) +44 (0)1865 240 941 or (e-mail) info@wiley-capstone.co.uk

Contents

Introduction to ExpressExec

ExpressExec is an innovative new concept in business publishing. It provides a practical, new resource for those in business wanting to check, develop and fine-tune their approaches and techniques in an ever-changing, fast-track world. You want to maximize your business and executive performance. How do these titles help?

First, let's be clear what they are *not*. They are not conventional business texts describing in detail how to undertake an activity, area of work or management function, though they do act as a guide to such references and encapsulate key approaches. Rather they are designed to act as a catalyst to analysis, thinking and decision. They will provide help to practicing managers who want to review a topic, fast, in a way that spans every aspect of it and links to action based on the new realities.

Thus *ExpressExec* texts:

» put their topics in *context* within the whole canvas of business activity;
» *position* their subject, showing how it developed and how it is affected by global trends, the information technology revolution and other developments;

» *explain and comment* to address the key issues affecting achieving success in today's world;
» *exemplify* and illustrate, through examples and case studies, showing how to link approaches and decisions to best current practice; and
» *link to the future*, making it easier to decide on the way forward and anticipate further changes that will impact business development.

Overall the intention is to assist you to keep up to date and to address issues for action in a practical manner. The information presented here constitutes a resource that is relevant in a dynamic world, and which acts as a firm foundation for future consideration and action.

Introduction

» A means to an end
» A changing world

"If you want a hamster, you start by asking for a pony."
Annabel, age 6, posted on the Internet

The youngster quoted above apparently has some inherent knowledge or insight into the process of negotiating. It may stand her in good stead in later life because negotiating – bargaining to put it simply – is used in so many different contexts in both private and organizational life.

Negotiating, the process of making a deal and agreeing the terms on which it is arranged, is an important, and ubiquitous business skill. It is essentially:

» *An interactive communication skill*, one that must be deployed in many different circumstances and at every level of organizational life.

It is a close partner of sales skills, that is as much used on the other side of the sales process, in purchasing, and may need to be utilized in a wide variety of business dealings from union negotiation to corporate take-over and merger arrangements.

» *A career skill*, in the sense that it is one of those skills – along with a number of others including being able to present formally, write a good report and manage their time – that many (perhaps most) people working in an organization need.

These skills are not only necessary in doing a job successfully, but also are needed if someone is to be seen as fully competent; excelling in these areas enhances the likelihood of career success (for more details see the ExpressExec volume on *Career Management*). Negotiation may also be needed to obtain the best deal – and remuneration package – for yourself.

Good negotiators are in a strong position to make a good impression and a good deal.

A MEANS TO AN END

A great deal can be riding on the outcome of a negotiation. Success can make money, save time or secure your future (and your reputation). To negotiate and do so successfully is to deploy a technique that can work positively for you in a host of different ways. The overall deal you strike may be vital, and individual elements of it can be significant, perhaps very significant. For example, without a little negotiation regarding the delivery date for the manuscript for this work, I could not have taken it on and would have missed the opportunity that writing it provides for me.

The techniques of negotiating are many and varied. It needs the right approach, the right attitude and attention to a multitude of details on the way through. Like so many business skills it cannot be applied by rote; its use must be tailored - intelligently tailored - to the individual circumstances on a case by case basis. It has elements of being an adversarial process about it and it needs handling with care. Individual techniques may be common sense in some ways, but they need deploying with some sensitivity. You can as easily find that someone is running rings around you as that you are tying up the deal of a lifetime.

In this work negotiating is explained and investigated. The way it works is spelt out and the process is illustrated in a variety of ways and in different contexts. The book shows that it is not only important to be able to negotiate, but also to be able to plan and manage the process in order to increase the likelihood of achieving the outcome you want.

A CHANGING WORLD

Finally here it should be said that negotiating is a front-line skill. It puts those undertaking it in an exposed position. It may involve people within the same organization or outside it; much negotiating is traditionally between supplier and buyer. Whatever the precise purpose of negotiating, it is affected by the increasingly dynamic and competitive world in which organizations operate. For example, buyers negotiating arrangements with suppliers have considerable power and there is always a competitor waiting in the wings to pick up the pieces if a supplier fails to make a deal that is acceptable. Such competitive pressure also exists internally within an organization and can affect all sorts of negotiation.

However much it may be a skill that needs to be deployed widely around an organization, and one which many people should aim to have as a technique in their armory, it is certainly a high-level one. Senior management and leaders of many kinds must be good negotiators. If the skill is one that "goes with the territory" for you, then there is real danger in failing to get to grips with it; and real opportunity for those who make it their stock in trade.

What is Negotiating?

"There are two fools in every market place. One asks too little, the other asks too much."

Traditional Russian proverb

Negotiating is a complex process. At least it is complex in the sense that it is an interactive process that involves a multitude of techniques. Perhaps the greatest complexity is that of orchestrating the overall process, managing it within the context of a meeting. The purpose of negotiating is however clear.

NEGOTIATING DEFINED

Negotiating is a special form of communication. Thus it is best defined in that context. Communication is the basic process, the flow of information between people that informs, instructs and more. More important here is *persuasive communication.* This is designed to produce agreement and action in another person; as such this may have a wealth of applications including selling where the agreement is to buy something.

When persuasion has worked and agreement is there, at least in principle, negotiation may take over. It is concerned with the relationship between two parties where the needs of both are largely in balance. It is the process of *bargaining* that arranges and agrees the basis on which agreement will be concluded – the terms and conditions under which the deal will be struck.

Consider a simple example. In the classic case of wage bargaining, the employer wants to reach an agreement (to secure the workforce and keep the business running), and the employees want an agreement (so that the process of negotiating is over, and they can get on with earning at a new, improved, rate). This process of balance defines the process. In selling, the first stage is to get agreement – from the point of view of the seller *to get what they want* – but beyond that, negotiating is what *decides the "best deal."* Thus if you are buying a car, say, then the things that need arrangement are all those making up the "package" which goes beyond just the car itself. Such factors may include: the finance, discounts, extras to be included with the car (air-conditioning, perhaps) that are not standard, delivery, trade in of an existing vehicle etc. The applications of negotiating are wide; see box.

THE APPLICATION OF NEGOTIATING

Negotiating is used:

» as part of the sales process (by both buyer and seller);
» between individuals for primarily personal reasons (e.g. negotiating a pay increase or remuneration package or "discussing" with your spouse where to go on holiday);
» in wage bargaining (as between an employer organization and a union or staff group);
» in political circles (as in treaties between governments);
» internationally (either between individuals or organizations in different countries or literally on a world wide basis – like the recent talks about measures to combat global warming); and
» in corporate affairs (takeovers, mergers and a variety of alliances and collaborations, sought or forced by circumstances).

It often involves a financial element (though it may not) and can involve two people or groups of people and take place at every level of an organizational hierarchy. Finally it may be momentary and minor – *if you can deputize for me at tomorrow's meeting, I can give you a little longer on that deadline we spoke about,* but still need getting right.

The nature of negotiating

Negotiating is characterized by various factors.

» It is an interactive and balanced process and one where the outcome must, by definition, be agreeable to both parties (though that does not mean both parties will necessarily regard the outcome as ideal); this is usually referred to as the win-win factor.
» An adversarial element is inherent within the process as each party vies to get the best deal that they can. Keep in mind sayings like that of Ashleigh Brilliant – *"I always win. You always lose. What could be fairer than that?"* This aspect must be kept in check; if it gets out of hand, negotiations may deteriorate into a slanging match with

both parties making demands to which neither will ever agree, so that the whole process is stillborn.

» A major part of the process of bargaining is one of *trading*; in other words as the terms and conditions are discussed – the variables as they are called – they must be traded to create a balance on an *if I agree to this, you will need to let me have that* basis (more of this core process is described in Chapter 6 The State of the Art).

» A fair amount of give and take is necessary, and the to and fro discussion takes time; negotiating cannot be rushed (this is particularly so in some cultures, see Chapter 5 The Global Dimension).

» A ritual element is involved, that is negotiating must be seen to be doing justice to the task it addresses; time is one element of this, as are a variety of procedural matters.

THE CORE ELEMENTS

The process of negotiating involves juggling with three key factors: information, time and power. Consider these in turn.

» *Information*: the old saying that information is power is certainly true in negotiation. Both parties want to know as much as possible about the other – the person (or people), their needs, priorities, intention and approach. A better understanding on one side or the other allows a more accurate deployment of the skills and gives that side an incontrovertible advantage.

» *Time*: this is always a pressure and urgency and specific deadlines may be imposed on any situation, often coming from outside the control of the person negotiating. For example, someone's boss may be imposing tight timing (for reasons explained or unexplained). Similarly, circumstances may affect timing, for example in the way the publication of a company's annual accounts – announcing record results – might make concluding a pay deal ahead of the announcement a priority for management. On the other hand, time and timing is one of the raw materials of most negotiations and it is said, with some truth, that there has not been a deadline in history that was not negotiable.

» *Power*: many factors can add weight – power – to the ability to negotiate. The phrase about "having someone over a barrel" picks up this point, it means power is very much on one side. Power stems form two main areas.

  » *The power of precedent*: this is the equivalent of the "self-fulfilling prophesy" – we know something cannot be done because a certain past experience tells us so. The result? We avoid even raising an issue and the power moves to the other side. Negotiating demands an open mind, a thorough search for everything that might assist – taking a chance or a risk is part of the process and doing so and addressing every possibility regardless of precedent gives us power and improves the chances of success.

  » *The power of legitimacy*: this is power projected by authority. People's attitudes to what can be negotiated come, in part, from where and how they see something originate. For example, even something as simple as a form or a notice is often taken as gospel. Checking into a hotel, how many people do other than fill in the complete registration form? Very few; most take it as a given that it must be done, yet, in my experience, if you ask, then often a few key details are sufficient.

The point here is that the authority may be real or it may be *assumed or implied*. In other words power is intentionally invested in something to give it more power and make it weigh more heavily in the balance. This may be very minor. Someone says – *that would be against policy* – and suddenly someone else feels less able to challenge it. Even when both parties understand this, the principle still adds an additional element to discussions, which all the time must assess the real power being brought to the table as the meeting proceeds.

A CONSTRUCTIVE PROCESS

Before concluding this brief introduction it is worth looking at things from the other side and considering what negotiating is not. It is not an argument. A complaint makes a good example. Say your fridge is acting like a microwave oven and you go into the shop that supplied it to state your grievance. That is not negotiating either. It may produce an apology, but what you want is action. There are numbers of things that could be done (ranging from swapping it for a new machine today, no questions asked, to getting in touch with the manufacturer, the latter implying a delay of indeterminate length). The mix of action, timing, recompense etc. needs negotiating.

So negotiating demands that proposals are made and discussed. In the simple example above, negotiating can fail not because it is done badly but because it is avoided and not done at all. The situation is then likely to turn acrimonious and argument is all that ensues.

At the end of the day all the parties to negotiation need to understand its nature. It may be adversarial, but we are aiming at a mutually agreeable outcome – what is usually referred to as a *win-win outcome*. If one party goes headlong for the best deal regardless, the likelihood is that they will push the other into a corner and that they will feel unable to agree to anything; the negotiation stalls. If both parties accept that some compromise is necessary, then the outcome is likely to be better for both. Thus negotiating is about seeking common ground, relating to the other person and their concerns, participating in to and fro debate, but not insisting on a totally rigid agenda. It means asking questions – and *listening* to the answers, disclosing information (to some extent), openly stating a point of view, building a relationship and treating the other person with respect.

Negotiating must aim throughout at agreement and actively act to avoid stalemate. If persuasion answers the question *will this person agree?* – then negotiating must address the question *on what basis will this person agree?*

KEY INSIGHTS

The overview set out here shows that understanding and utilizing negotiation requires:

» a basis of sound, effective communications skills (because nego-tiating is a specialist form of communications);
» an understanding of the role of negotiating (because it is almost always part of a broader picture, for instance one that starts with persuasion);

» the ability to orchestrate a plethora of techniques and relate what is done to the particular meeting and circumstances (in other words this is not something that can be applied by rote); and

» a sensitivity to the people involved as what is done must be based on an understanding of them and their needs.

The Evolution of Negotiating

» Long-term business trends
» New realities in the market place
» The power of major accounts
» Training
» Summary

"Negotiation is a field of knowledge and endeavor that focuses on gaining the favor of people from whom we want things. It is that simple."

Herb Cohen, author You Can Negotiate Anything

Man was doubtless negotiating in caves at the dawn of time - *sure, I can let you have some mammoth steaks, but only if you help me cut up the mammoth.* It is a perennial technique and a close partner of persuasion and selling. Many authors refer to it in this way, for example:

"It's hard to imagine business - or even life - without negotiation. Practically every business interaction, from the largest corporate merger to a meeting to decide the site of a new bicycle shed, depends on negotiation. In fact, it's rare to find any human transaction at all where there isn't some room for discussion and modification of terms.

The good negotiator has to call on a whole raft of skills. He or she needs to be an effective communicator, combining the abilities to sell and to listen. The negotiator must be able to balance tactical and strategic considerations. Good negotiators know their business and their company inside out - and know just as much about the other side too. As if this isn't enough, good negotiators also need flexibility - the ability to explore what is possible, changing goal from a hypothetical summit to a more reachable hill."

B. Clegg Instant Negotiation *(Kogan Page).*

Thus reviewing its long-term history is not likely to be of great use. There are however a number of factors that make the need to negotiate well, much more pressing than in the past and these are worth review.

LONG TERM BUSINESS TRENDS

All the main trends affecting businesses and organizations over recent years (and not so recent, for that matter) affect the likely need for, and importance of, negotiation. The main factors are as follows.

» *Financial pressures*: taxation, interest rates, more pressure on cash flow and more pressure from shareholders, banks and any other stakeholder involved (including staff, who always want a greater slice of the pie) – all highlight any situation that affects the key financial ratios. Thus, for example, margins are protected more fiercely in negotiating with suppliers and, to take a wholly different example, a harder line is taken with union demands.

» *Administrative burdens*: largely, so the conventional wisdom has it, government inspired. Whatever the truth of that, paperwork – from matters linked to employment law to the provision of information and compliance with edicts of all sorts – does take up significant time; and as yet the long-awaited "paperless office" is nowhere in sight. Anything threatening to increase this burden is resisted. This might mean negotiating with a supplier simply to create a smoother administrative process between supplier and supplied, or again negotiations designed to make or save money in light of what is perceived as being spent on (perhaps unnecessary) administration.

» *Competition*: market conditions seem to get more and more competitive; and international competition is a major factor in this picture. This in turn increases risk, reduces margins and creates an attitude that anywhere that might produce (or save) money must be pursued hard.

» *Technology*: of all sorts, and information technology in particular, is a wonder of the age. There is no doubt that it brings major efficiency and convenience; but it also brings cost, a steep learning curve and an apparently built-in obsolescence that means many people feel they are on a technological rollercoaster and there is always something new to get to grips with. Again, although it can be a route to financial savings, costs are perceived as growing and financial criteria assume greater priorities.

In fact all the trends and processes affecting business can have implications that lead to more hard-nosed attitudes about money and tougher negotiations. Environmental factors are now more important; and more costly. Government restrictions also tend to prompt higher costs (e.g. complying with more stringent safety regulations). Beyond all this attitudes change; many of those working in an organization are so used to the concept of getting a good deal, questioning what is offered and negotiating, that it has become a reflex. It occurs in one area for good practical reasons and then those who must exercise negotiating skills there, deploy them wherever else possible – after all the fact that praise is collected for a good deal done easily tends to keep the trend for more negotiation going.

NEW REALITIES IN THE MARKET PLACE

So many markets have had economic difficulties, if not outright recession, in recent years that this has inevitably had an effect on the attitudes and therefore on the practices of managers affected by them. As one prime application of negotiating is linked to sales, this makes a good example. In recent years buyers are likely to:

» use a greater number of suppliers (perhaps playing them off against each other);
» be better informed and check more details in advance of discussions;
» want to take less risk;
» be more demanding (of service, quality and whatever they describe as "value for money");
» think, and make decisions, on a shorter term basis;
» delay decisions (or simply not buy for a period – *replacing the company cars can be held over until next year*);
» reduce stock levels held;
» want more formal arrangements – *put it in writing*;
» be less loyal to suppliers; and
» want longer credit, pay later – or both.

This is a list that might be added to; certainly an overall increased toughness is likely to be in evidence in a number of ways, including things where detailed negotiations are now necessary, when in the past a reasonable package might have been accepted without question.

Whatever the specifics involved here, a new breed of buyer has evolved, all of whom – whatever their own individual reasons – make much tougher negotiating adversaries.

THE POWER OF MAJOR ACCOUNTS

There is a specific category of buyers worth an individual mention, those within key or major accounts. The relevant point here is one of power. In so many industries the share of markets is spread across fewer and fewer potential customers; in fast-moving consumer goods, product manufacturers in many countries find that there only four or five major suppliers with perhaps 80% of the market or more between them. The need to sell to them is high; lose one and a major part of the market is lost, and thus they wield considerable power. They are in a strong position to secure the deal they want and a long list of variables needs to be thrashed out with them before a deal can be struck; and all of these concern cost and reflect directly on profitability. The boxed paragraph below sets out some examples.

POWERFUL MAJOR CUSTOMERS

The kinds of thing – all variables – that a manufacturer might be pressed on by a major customer include:

» additional time from the field sales force (for instance to help merchandising);
» discounts (and there may be many different bases for them, e.g. quantity bought or when purchase is made; and some are retrospective);
» any special packaging and packing;
» delivery (maybe to multiple locations), labeling, credit terms (and beyond);
» returns and damage arrangements;
» advertising and promotional support;
» merchandising materials;
» training of customers' staff; and
» financing (including special credit terms).

These sorts of cost are, of course, all in addition to normal production and distribution costs. Yet major players can make demands here that quickly put margins under pressure, knowing that the pressure for the supplier to maintain a relationship with them is intense.

On the other side, a buyer – say a retailer – does not want to alienate a supplier and miss the opportunity of profiting from selling a good product. So realistically a balance is necessary; it is however one that the supplier may sometimes think is tending to be one sided. Whatever else, in most developed markets it dictates that negotiation takes place.

TRAINING

In the 1970s and 1980s there was a period of considerably increased training activity, as it became accepted that a greater professionalism would help improve company results. This was true across the board of many management techniques and nowhere was this more evident than in marketing. Sales and allied skills such as negotiating were favored topics. For a while at that time sales and marketing people had an edge; they tended to be better versed in the techniques and practices of negotiating.

This quickly changed and buyers became just as likely as sellers to have a good grounding in negotiating skills.

Nowadays the way to proceed is twofold.

» First, the only assumption to make about an unknown adversary in negotiating is that they are likely to be professional, well briefed and skilful.
» Second, you must be sure that you are as well versed as possible yourself (See Chapter 9 for details of available training).

As Chapters 6 and 7 show, there is much to get to grips with about negotiation. Experience is valuable, but it is doubly valuable if it is building on a firm foundation of understanding.

KEY INSIGHTS
The key things of value from considering the background and history here are that:

» the pressure to negotiate and do a good deal are great (on both parties);
» this pressure is tending to increase as competitiveness in all its forms increases; and
» you should never underestimate either your adversary or the nature of the negotiating process itself; concluding a satisfactory deal is dependent on deploying a series of skills, professionally and effectively, and making them work harder than does the other party involved.

The E-Dimension

"Make a suggestion or assumption and let them tell you you're wrong. People also have a need to feel smarter than you are."
Mark McCormack, author What they don't teach you at Harvard Business School

The revolution of computers, information technology and the "e" prefix that now links to almost everything has had a profound impact on business. As the *ExpressExec* series shows, some areas of business have been changed in a way that affects the whole way business is conducted.

In this instance, as the nature of negotiating is a process of personal, interactive communication, it must still be applied in a discussion which is, most usually, face to face. As such the e-dimension is here not the most important element of the process. There are however several ways in which it exerts influence and where it is as well to be aware of the effects that may be experienced.

THE BLUR FACTOR

One thing is for sure, the world has speeded up in recent years. It may still turn on its axis every 24 hours, but for those in business everything seems to happen quicker. There is more to do, there are more (and tighter) deadlines, and there is certainly more information to be assessed and acted on than ever in the past. The relationship between time, quality and cost is something everyone has to juggle with – think of it graphically as three factors joined in a triangle by elastic; each is pulling the triangle out of shape and decisions constantly have to be made about a compromise between them (Fig. 4.1).

An American author is quoted as commenting on this struggle with the words – *They didn't want it right, they wanted it Wednesday.* Many people will identify with this phrase.

Pressure on time is a regularly used ploy in negotiating. You need to be on your guard and must not allow yourself to be programmed to rate sheer speed so highly that other factors go out the window. As has been said elsewhere, there is not a deadline in history that was not negotiable. Equally you may be able to use the (perhaps apparent) pressure of time as a ploy to assist your own side of things. It is, for example, a fact that, despite the speed with which computers operate, they are regularly

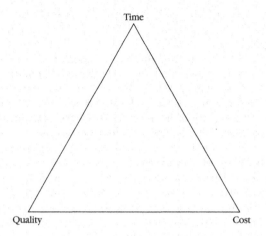

Fig. 4.1 Relationship between time, quality and cost.

used as an excuse for delay – *we'll have to run that through the computer – the system was down this morning, I can let you have details tomorrow*. This has become such a well-known element of modern life that it is rarely questioned; it is a fact that can be used (carefully) in discussions to good effect, and something to question in others.

IMPERSONAL COMMUNICATIONS

One particular area that now operates at unprecedented speed is that of certain types of communication. E-mails go at 3000 miles a second and, for the most part, people expect a prompt reply. Alongside this a range of "new" communications methods now carry a significant proportion of business communications; such include: mobile phones, answer phones and voicemail, videoconferencing and teleconferencing, text messages, multi-media communications etc.

Much negotiating is, of course, face to face. Indeed much of it is best conducted face to face, but other methods are necessary, if only as a single part of the overall transaction. Consider face to face communications for a moment. Much of the information that moves to and fro is enhanced (and sometimes diluted) by visual signals.

Messages can easily be reinforced by checking, repetition, clarification and discussion; by all the to and fro interaction of people dealing directly with each other.

Other forms of communication, whether sending a written proposal or an e-mail, are not like this. They are certainly fast, but they are less personal, they prohibit visual signals and may lack "quality." As an illustration of this last point consider the difference between a letter and an e-mail. One looks good (provided you have a well designed letterhead). It gives the impression that some trouble has been taken and projects a fuller image of the writer. The e-mail does not look good, may follow a much less formal style and not give anything like the same impression of quality. Like many people I am sure, I find that many very brief e-mails that I receive are not precisely clear. Further communications must sometimes go to and fro maybe several times before both parties are clear. With many things this matters little (though it can be annoying and time consuming); with negotiation such lack of immediate precision may matter a great deal.

So, with this in mind consider the following.

» Plan communications carefully, taking time as necessary to get them right.
» Select the communication method carefully and in light of all the elements that make one method different from another. Consider: How important is speed? How important is clarity, image etc.? Not everything is best the electronic way, though on other occasions the speed of e-mail – or of actually conducting a conversation on line in real time – may be paramount. Sometimes too it is useful to take two bites at the apple: an e-mail is confirmed by post in a different form.
» Recognize any limitations, especially of a lack of visual clues. These can sometimes be overcome (you can e-mail the graph that will explain those figures in an instant, for example), but sometimes things that would be possible face to face must wait until that is possible. Be careful, remember that for all your verbal powers some things are just not possible in words only (try explaining to someone – rather than showing them – something like how to tie a shoelace!).
» Check that the right message has got across, especially when you have to use the fast route.

We have more options for communications now than at any time in the past. We can set up conference calls, we can make them video conference calls, we can sit at our computer and see on screen something that someone wants to explain to us as they do so, and we can respond faster than ever to messages that come to us in a plethora of different ways. However, the responsibility for getting a message right, for making the communication work, remains with the communicator. *You* have to make the right communications choice, plan and execute it to achieve a precision of understanding and not be seduced into thinking that because a few lines on the e-mail is easiest it is also always best. Remember one characteristic of the e-mail – it can be deleted in a split second with one click of the mouse.

GREATER KNOWLEDGE

Something else that the wired world makes possible is that of increased knowledge. The people with whom you negotiate are likely to be not just well informed, but better informed that ever before. What is more, they can get into a position of being well informed faster and more easily than ever before. For example, the job of getting some background about an organization anywhere in the world may take no more than a few minutes logged onto the Internet. Such time can also quickly provide information about competitive organizations or products.

This fact should always be borne in mind. Do not underestimate people with whom you negotiate, or operate on the basis of unwarranted assumptions about their level of knowledge; at best it may make you look silly, at worst you may lose advantage and perhaps the whole deal.

There is a positive side of this that is picked up under the next heading.

SUPPORT MATERIALS

Linking to the previous point, those with whom you negotiate need information and in many ways part of what you need to do is to supply this. New technology can help with this in a variety of ways. Information can be provided ahead of a meeting, during a meeting and afterwards if necessary. The following examples give the feel of what is possible, you can:

» show visual aids, long distance, by placing information on a computer screen in front of someone so that you can talk about it together;
» have a laptop computer in a meeting and show supporting information to someone overlooking your screen (and print it off for them or zap it to their machine electronically);
» use a PowerPoint presentation to enhance what you are saying; and
» deploy more sophisticated displays – for example a virtual tour of a building, or a computer-generated image of a product yet to be made.

The possibilities here are many and varied, but there is also a significant caveat here. Whatever you use from this sort of list of possibilities, it must work properly. Even with something as routine as a PowerPoint presentation now is, I reckon that one in three of those that I view fail in some way. For example, at a recent one every change of slide was delayed. The key was hit and then the change came only after three-quarters of a second. It did not seem worth stopping for, yet at the end of half an hour the audience cringed every time it happened. Any such failing can be just annoying for people, though that alone is to be avoided, or it can risk a serious dilution of understanding.

The strength of anything like this is enhanced when it is tailored. Show someone something and it may be useful, indeed it may impress. Show them something described as prepared *for them* (and explained as such) and it will be taken more seriously and also impress more.

MAKING A BOOKING

As a brief case in point I recently booked several rooms at a Marriott Hotel overseas. I found their Website, made contact and got a polite, informative and prompt reply. I queried, as you do, their first offer of the rate. At this point I found myself locked into a spiral of communication with first one, then two people in the sales office as e-mails went to and fro. Each reply was polite, but my questions were perpetually ignored. Perhaps it was a tactic to put me off negotiating. It did not do that; it very nearly put me off making the booking at all. Finally the questions were answered, offers were made in both directions and a deal was struck which seemed satisfactory to both parties.

Here the methodology made getting in contact and getting replies fast, but it seemed to dilute understanding as assumptions were made and matters (as I saw it) went unread or ignored. Service quality was certainly diluted and, because of the image I now have of them, other people at the hotel will have a bigger job to do when I arrive to make sure I see it in a good light – maybe good enough to go back or recommend it to others.

KEY INSIGHTS

This is an area of change. Information technology is changing people's attitudes to many things. It is also providing an apparently unending succession of new ways of doing things. Just because something is technically possible does not mean it is automatically useful, and certainly not that it is automatically universally useful. But this is an area to watch. You should:

» keep up to date with the possibilities;
» check them out, not least so that you can use appropriate ones faultlessly;
» deploy them judiciously only where they will help what you are trying to do, be appreciated and found helpful by those with whom you are negotiating, and maybe also act to impress;
» assess their usefulness, refine their actual use and learn from initial experiences to make later use more effective; and
» replace them, as necessary, when they are overtaken by better ways, even though you are now used to them and the learning curve demands that some time is spent on achieving change.

The Global Dimension

"A negotiator should observe everything. You must be part Sherlock Holmes, part Sigmund Freud."

Victor Kyam, author and CEO Remington Products

For so many people today's market is a global market. Many managers and others find travel is a regular part of their activity and that people in a variety of countries are their regular contacts. English is the business language of the world, but that does not mean that every contact and every communication can be handled in an identical fashion around the world.

As is explained elsewhere (Chapters 2 and 6 particularly) negotiation is a complex process. It is an interactive, personal skill, and it is applied in many areas where there is a great deal hanging on its outcome. Meetings may be lengthy. Many details need to be addressed and the precision that the process demands is considerable. The end result is often a contract and that is something that certainly must be the result of precision and mutual understanding.

DEALING WITH DIFFERENCE

A host of difficulties are likely to occur in conversations across cultural, national and linguistic divides. Consider one well known example. The Japanese use the word "Yes" (Hai) not only to mean yes, but just as likely to mean "I'm listening," "Right," "I see," "Understood" and more. They avoid the word "No" (Lai) in order not to offend, so a translation of "No" is likely to be something like "Let's look at this further." If they really want to express a negative then the most likely word to be used is "Difficult." And that is just a couple of words in two languages!

Experts on negotiation from all fields agree on the importance of such difficulty. For example B. Clegg in his book *Instant Negotiation* (Kogan Page) refers to culture shock and says:

"Time and time again, cultural differences have caused problems in negotiations. Anything, from how the other stakeholders are addressed to how much price haggling is allowed and expected, will have cultural variants. Cultural differences will bring in different expectations, difficulties in communication and differences in attitude to timing. It might be, for instance, that representatives of two cultures are meeting for the first time for a social event on the evening before a formal negotiation. One culture might expect to have early discussions on the subject of the negotiation. The other might expect to stick to social niceties. This second group would find the first pushy, while the first would find their opponents evasive. Neither is doing anything wrong, apart from not anticipating the other's cultural reaction."

Other texts are geared predominantly, or exclusively, to cross-cultural negotiating. In *Cross Cultural Business Negotiations* (D.W. Hendon, R.A. Hendon and P. Herbig, Quorum Books) cultural influences in negotiation are described thus:

"All human interactions are, by definition, intercultural. When two individuals meet, it is an intercultural encounter since they both have different (sometimes drastically different, if not opposite) ways to perceive, discover, and create reality. All negotiations are therefore intercultural. Negotiations with a boss, spouse, child, friend, fellow employee, union representative, official from a foreign country, and so on are all intercultural loaded. In some countries, negotiating is present in practically every transaction, from settling a taxi fare to buying bread. Intercultural negotiations do not only exist because people who think, feel, and behave differently have to reach agreements on practical matters such as how to produce, consume, organize and distribute power, and grant rewards, but because of the very nature of the challenging, unpredictable, and contradictory world we live in. We are forced to negotiate.

In every negotiation (domestic or international), the participants have different points of view and different objectives.

When you are negotiating with someone from your own country, it is often truly possible to expedite communications by making reasonable cultural assumptions. The situation reverses itself when two cultures are involved. Making assumptions about another culture is often counterproductive since it can too often lead to misunderstandings and miscommunications. The international negotiator must be careful not to allow cultural stereotypes to determine his or her relations with local businesspersons. Needs, values, interests and expectations may differ dramatically.

What gives a person his or her identity no matter where he or she was born is his or her culture – the total communication framework. Culture is a set of shared and enduring meanings, values, and beliefs that characterize national, ethnic, or other groups and orient their behavior. Culture directs judgment and opinion, describes the criteria for what is good or bad. Language structures reality and orders experience. Culture is the property of a society, it is acquired through acculturation or socialization by the individual from the society, and it subsumes every area of social life. The language of an individual significantly influences his or her perceptions and thoughts. Culture may be an obstacle to the extent that cultural stereotypes and differences distort signals and cause misunderstandings.''

The moral is simple: forewarned is forearmed and if you negotiate in multi-cultural situations you need to do your homework.

Let us be clear. Negotiating demands that we:

» "read" people to try and identify their attitude and position at any particular point in the proceedings;
» anticipate what may occur and what line people may take as things progress; and
» match what we do to the precise state that the other party is in at the time.

Cross-cultural meetings

All the above are, in turn, dependent on clear understanding, and all this may be different – and perhaps more difficult – in cross-cultural meetings. We may recognize the fact, but responding to it still needs conscious effort and the problem is one of what is called expectation. We grow up through a multitude of experiences and all of them are used, semi-automatically, to predict how the future will be; it is a process that gives us an expectation. For example, if you are asked to a dinner party or a cocktail party then you believe that, broadly at least, you know how it will be. Certainly you know something about how prompt you should be in attending, what you should and should not wear, how you should conduct yourself and so on. Normally too, at least in your own environment, your expectation will be broadly correct.

But in unfamiliar circumstances - in negotiating with a foreign buyer, say - your expectation of many things can be either wrong or murky. You have to remain open-minded and plan to be quick on your feet so that you can try to respond appropriately even as you learn fast how things are going to be. Clearly any checking, research or briefing you can undertake in advance will be an asset. It enables you to deal with the situation better, it prevents you making real gaffes and it may give you an edge over colleagues or adversaries who have taken less trouble and are therefore less well briefed.

A number of factors (in no particular order) are worth bearing in mind.

» *Language*: although English is to a large extent the universal language of business, those whose first language is English still need to exercise some caution in dealing with those for whom it is not. For example:
  » *speak a little slower than normal*: though not so slowly as to sound patronizing;
  » *be careful and precise in your use of language*: to ensure accurate meaning is transferred, consider restricting vocabulary a little;
  » *signpost clearly*: that is be sure to say what is coming and the nature of it - *let me give you an example*; *an important point is*; and
  » *verify understanding as you go*: again do not overdo it, but an occasional remark like - *am I making that clear?* - is useful. *Note*: if discussions are being translated special care is necessary and it is worthwhile to discuss how it will be done, with the translator ahead of the main discussion.
» *Beginnings*: be particularly careful about the introductions and greetings, things like careful exchange of business cards (in the East), eye contact (not too long at first in the Middle East, and not with women) and not flinching from a Russian bear hug can be important.

» *Appearance*: this is largely a matter of common sense, though if you are taken out it may be worth checking what is appropriate in advance.

» *Manners*: this can be something of a minefield; you may need to find out whether you need to eat the sheep's eyes in the Middle East and know that it is rude to cross your legs and point your feet at someone in Thailand. Just the appropriate level of familiarity needs checking; the French for instance tend to be more formal than most people and Monsieur/Madame need to be used regularly. Equally you must not be unnecessarily offended by, say, the Chinese who can be very abrupt as a matter of course – *No, that's wrong!* – without meaning it quite as it would be taken if put that way in the West.

» *Body language*: the signs given in another culture may be confusing. In Bulgaria a nodded head means disagreement and shaking the head means agreement, in Korea too much smiling is taken as someone being pushy.

» *Humour*: careful! It may not travel, too much may be seen as inappropriately frivolous, but on the other hand you probably do not want to come over as too serious in some circumstances.

» *Timing*: attitudes to time vary around the world. Punctuality has different degrees of importance around the world. More important, some cultures just take longer over some things. In America the culture is very much one of "getting down to business" fast; elsewhere, in the East for instance, preliminaries are important and time just to get to know each other a little is taken routinely.

Even tiny details may matter. For example Americans write the date: 12-15-02, i.e. with the month first. In Britain it is usually the reverse. Certainly this needs getting right before you agree a delivery date. Matters to do with everyday things may cause problems too. Take meal times, if you dine in Japan it is likely to be early (6/7 p.m.), with an Italian it will be late (9/10 p.m.) – getting this kind of detail wrong can offend.

As relationships grow, perhaps if you are meeting and doing business regularly, a wider set of circumstances needs to be taken into account and planned for – entertaining, for example.

Whether you are traveling to other parts of the world, or dealing with people who travel to you, some care in all these ways is sensible.

Certainly it is important not to stereotype people or make assumptions; and this is easy to do when your experience of something is limited.

MEASURING THE DIFFERENCE

It may be useful not simply to resolve to remember that cultures differ, but to measure the differences, especially that between your own and one with which you need to deal. John Mattock, who runs Lyddon-Mattock Associates, has devised a model that incorporates many ideas into one matrix which enables you to run a slide rule, as it were, over specific cultural differences. It measures 18 factors on a scale from one to six under three main headings: Perception and Cognition, Self and Society, and Decisions and Communication. The device enables you to highlight key differences likely to affect relationships and communications, and to see this against a background summarizing the broad picture (there is more of this in Chapters 8 and 9).

A case in point

Here, just to illustrate the range of things to be borne in mind, we consider one country, albeit one that is alien to many: Japan. Japanese business people tend to be well traveled, are group orientated and rather formal in their dealings with each other. To get off to a good start in negotiations with the Japanese you should:

» not overdo eye contact;
» shake hands only if a hand is offered to you (and *do not* try to bow in Japanese style, though a sincere nod of the head is appreciated);
» use titles with names; and
» make sure that careful use of language ensures understanding - checking as necessary.

Business cards are much used (yours should have a Japanese translation on the reverse).

Details may be widely checked. You quote a delivery date and they will want to speak to those involved in implementing it to reassure themselves that it is seen as possible. The Japanese go to considerable lengths to conceal their emotions, hate losing face, and are uncomfortable if others (you) lose control, for instance showing anger or impatience. Respect and patience are to be displayed and any negotiating is, in part, seen as a pursuit of harmony.

Language will always need to be used carefully and you should not act immediately to fill silences, as taking a moment over things is normal. Politeness and consideration is valued, and personal touches (things like a thank you note, or small gifts – ask before unwrapping if it is given to you) are seen as very much part of building relationships.

Specifically in negotiating: considerable detail is expected about any matter being discussed. An overview or seemingly vague or disorganized information will be read with suspicion as evasion. Good support material – anything from plans and graphs to summaries of details dealt with – is appreciated, indeed expected. As the Japanese will most likely deal with you as a group – it is unusual to deal with a single person, you must relate to the whole group, even those taking less part or less able to speak English (if that is the language being used). The differences here, certainly with a Western approach, are considerable and even a snapshot like this is sufficient to show that a good deal of checking is necessary and likely to pay dividends.

KEY INSIGHTS

Such a picture can quickly be used to flesh out a plan of action. Specific factors may be necessary:

» allowing a longer time than would be necessary elsewhere;
» more thorough preparation (for example to be able to express the necessary detail in a neat and logical form);
» research to get details about the people who will be involved; and
» having available – in advance – any gifts, and certainly appropriate and tailored support material that may be desirable.

All that said, and much of this example simply hints at a bigger picture, such factors are a separate and parallel dimension to everything else that is important about negotiating. Whatever culture you may deal with, some research and planning is probably going to be useful – as then are all the other principles that act to help make negotiating successful.

A FINAL WORD

Always remember that you will *never* know or understand as much about a nation or particular culture as those for whom it is "home." You need to recognize that you can go on learning and not allow yourself to come to a point where you think you know it all. It may surprise you when you make your umpteenth visit to a particular country and things still happen that cast just a little more light on how things work there. If you are open minded then this process will never stop; and every incidence of it can help make your next negotiation more successful.

The State of the Art

» Making the right deal: the process
» The nature of negotiating
» First things first
» The core element
» Added power
» Negotiating: the tactics
» Key techniques
» Interpersonal behavior
» Keeping on track
» Summary

"I love negotiating. It's creative. I love the feeling of seeing something and saying 'I can do something with this' and trying to get it. The anticipation of a successful conclusion is a wonderful feeling."
Phillipe Edmonds, businessman and former England cricketer

Marketing consists, in major part, of communication. One specialist form of personal communication, one that often goes hand in hand with selling, is that of negotiating. It can secure a deal, obtain the best financial outcome and provide the basis of good business relationships; but it must be done right.

The modern professional must be a technical expert in their chosen field. They must also often have management skills – of people and projects. And they must usually be effective in a range of personal skills including decision making, problem solving, time management and making a formal presentation. Many such skills are in the area of communications and are multipurpose; they can be used in communication internally as well as externally with clients and customers and a host of other contacts, people and bodies (e.g. unions). One such skill is negotiating. This chapter sets out to give an overview of how negotiating works, and does so in two main sections: first looking at the process, then at the tactics it involves.

1. MAKING THE RIGHT DEAL: THE PROCESS

Let us be clear. Negotiation and persuasion are different things. They are certainly interrelated: successful persuasion gains agreement to action (to agree a purchase, perhaps); negotiating is concerned with identifying, arranging and agreeing the terms and conditions that accompany agreement. Thus persuasion and agreement must logically come first. People do not waste time negotiating about something that they have no interest in. That is not to say that prior agreement is always openly stated; it may well not be – and in this way persuasive communication and negotiating merge with an imprecise line between them.

The nature of negotiating
Negotiating is a very particular process, characterized in a number of ways.

» First, it is complex. The complexity comes from the need to orchestrate a many faceted process rather than because of anything individually intellectually taxing. But you need to be quick on your feet, as it were, to keep all the necessary balls in the air, and always see the broad picture while concentrating on individual details.

» Second, while negotiating is not to be treated as an argument (if it is, then an impasse usually results), it *is* adversarial. Both parties involved want the best deal they can obtain. Yet compromise is essential: stick out for a perfect deal and the other party may walk away. Give way too easily and you may well regret what is then agreed. What is sought is usually referred to as a "win-win" outcome, one in which both parties are satisfied and, while they may not have what they would regard as the ideal "best deal," they do have an agreement with which they can feel comfortable.

» Third, there is a ritual aspect to negotiating. It is a process that needs to be gone through. It takes time. There is to and fro debate, and a mutually agreeable solution needs to be seen as being sought out as well as actually taking place. Too much haste, a rush for agreement or a take it or leave it approach can fail less because the deal it offers is unacceptable, more because the other party does not feel that the process is being taken seriously. They look for hidden meaning, they believe that something better must be possible and again the outcome can be stalemate.

Because of these factors the best negotiators are at pains to take the broad view, to understand the other person's point of view and what they are trying to achieve and why. Because the process of negotiating deals with a complex mix of issues and motivations, the way this is handled, not least the confidence with which this is done, is important. The negotiator who seems confident, has an ability to deal with all the issues logically and to manage the overall process, as well as picking up the detail, commands respect. How do you get on top of it all to this extent? Well, apart from having a clear understanding of the process, the key is preparation. It stands repeating: successful negotiation does not just happen; it is rarely possible to "wing it." Negotiating is not something most of us can make up as we go along. Remember the well-known saying of Abraham Lincoln: *"If I had nine hours to cut down a tree, I would spend six of them sharpening my axe."*

First things first

Successful negotiating begins with preparation. The rule here is simple. Do it. Preparation may only be a grand term for the age-old adage that it is best to engage the brain before the mouth, and it may take only a few minutes. Of course, at the other end of the scale it may mean sitting round the table with a few colleagues thrashing out exactly how to proceed with something. Whatever the necessary scale, the rule is that it should always happen.

It is particularly important to have clear objectives. If it is simply said that *we want the best deal possible* this provides nothing tangible with which to work. There is all the difference in the world between my *saying "let's see if the editor will pay me more for my next piece of text"* and setting out *to obtain a ten per cent increase in the fee*. Planning should be designed to produce the equivalent of a route map, something that helps shape the meeting. You know you cannot anticipate everything. With people it is just not possible to predict exactly what will happen. Your plan should, however, provide both an ideal route forward and a basis that will assist you if things do not go exactly to plan.

A final point here may also encourage you to spend a moment in preparation. You need to appear well prepared. If it is obvious you are not, if it seems you are unfamiliar with the issues – and more so if this is the case – then it is more likely someone will run rings round you. Preparation is the foundation to success and insurance against being outclassed.

Bearing all this in mind, it is logical that the choice of who will undertake negotiation in particular circumstances can also be important, just as, for instance, it makes a difference who will do best given a sales role.

The core element

The core of the negotiating process revolves around what are called *variables*: those factors that can be varied and arranged in different ways to create different potential deals. Thus in negotiating price for example, the price itself is clearly a variable, but discussion may involve associated matters such as payment terms, extras (e.g. with a product such might range from delivery to service arrangements to credit) and other factors such as timing and staffing; and more.

The overall rules here include:

» aiming for the best deal possible;
» discovering the full list of variables the other person has in mind;
» treating everything as a potential variable; and
» dealing with detail within the total picture (rather than one point at a time without reference to others).

Your use of the variables increases the power from which you deal. You can use them in various ways. You can prompt attention by offering reward: something you are prepared to give. Conversely you can offer punishment: by flagging your intention to withhold something. Your case is strengthened, given legitimacy in the jargon, by being supported by factual evidence, or by the use of bogeys, peripheral factors included only to distract or seek sympathy (e.g. statements such as – *that's beyond our control* – aiming to stop questioning in its tracks regardless of its truth).

You have to rank the variables, both in preparation and during the negotiating, when some fine-tuning may be necessary. There will be, at the very least, some things that are:

» essential: you cannot agree any deal without these points being part of it;
» ideal: what you intend to achieve (and the priorities, because there may be more of these than it is realistic to achieve); and
» tradable: in other words those things that you are prepared to give away to help create a workable deal.

The concept of trading variables is key to the whole process of negotiating. It is important never to give anything away. Concessions (that is variables given away) must be traded. For example a consultant might say – *we can certainly make sure all rail travel cost is second class, but we do need to add a little to the fees for the time taken.*

In doing this, the value of every concession must be maximized when you give it – and minimized when you accept it, so that the trading drives the balance in the direction you want. Thus saying: *I suppose I could do that, though it will make more work, but okay*, makes it seem that what you are agreeing is worth more than perhaps it actually is, while saying: *I would never normally do this*, implies that you are making an exception in their favor. Similarly saying: *Well, I suppose if I do that you won't need to* ... amplifies the effect that the concession seems to have for them. Clearly the way such things are said, perhaps incorporating a degree of exaggeration, in turn affects their reception.

Similarly with how you minimize the other parties' concessions. These can be

» dismissed – *Fine, now next* ... ;
» belittled – *Well, that's a small point out of the way*;
» amortized – *I suppose that saves a little each month*;
» taken for granted – *I would certainly expect that*; or
» otherwise reduced in power by the way they are accepted and referred to during the discussion.

So, the discussion has to be planned, directed and controlled. The confidence displayed during it is a significant factor (and links back to preparation). You must be clear about what you want to achieve. If you utilize every possible aspect of the discussion and treat everything as a variable, and deploy appropriate techniques to balance the whole picture and arrive at where you want to be (or somewhere close), then you will be able to achieve a reasonable outcome.

Remember the win-win scenario. The job is not to take people to the cleaners. If you are only prepared to agree something that is weighted heavily in your favor, then negotiating may break down and no agreement at all may be concluded. Sometimes you need to be prepared for this. There is often a minimum arrangement below which you are unprepared to go, and sometimes walking away rather than agreeing something you are not prepared to live with is the right decision.

Sometimes even if you have someone over the proverbial barrel a widely skewed deal is to be avoided. You need to think long term. What will screwing them into the ground make you look like? What are the future consequences of forced agreement? What may happen next time when you do not have quite so much strength to bring to the party?

Added power

Describing the process thus far has omitted one important aspect, and that is the individual techniques brought to bear. A confident negotiator may use a number of ploys to enhance what they do. Some are simple. For example, the use of silence, which many find embarrassing, to make a point or prompt a comment.

Too often someone will ask something like: *how important is this to you?* They wait a moment and then continue - *well, I'm sure it must be an important factor, now let's ...* They produce no real impact and, more important, no information by so doing; indeed silence may be joined by embarrassment. Wait. You can wait a long time if necessary (count to yourself to try this, you may well find that the pause that worries you, and makes you feel you must continue speaking if they will not, is only a few seconds; it just seems long). But using - really using - silence is one particularly significant ploy in negotiating.

This kind of element - negotiating tricks of the trade if you will - can enhance the process, turning a routine discussion into one that moves purposefully towards achieving your objectives.

2. NEGOTIATING – THE TACTICS

In the second part of this review of negotiating we now review ways of bringing control and power to what you do in aiming to strike a deal.

That negotiating is a complex process, certainly in the sense that there are many things to work at together if you are to make it go well, is clear. It was noted earlier that at its core it is an adversarial process, though balance is important and the concept of a "win-win" deal that both parties can walk away from with some satisfaction is important. Much of what must be done revolves around the trading of variables - a process of *if you will do this I will do that* - which must take place for an acceptable balance to be reached.

On the way, techniques and the careful deployment of various behavioral factors (with everything assisted by judicious preparation) can make or break your success.

Key techniques

With clear objectives in mind and an overall plan you can begin discussions. An agenda is sensible for any complex meeting. There is some merit in being the one that suggests one, albeit as something helpful to both parties. If you say something like: *We might find it best to* ... followed by an outline of how you want things to run (though *not*, of course, stating it as helpful to you) this sets the scene. Though it must be born in mind that this has something of the "laying all the cards on the table" feel to it, so you may want to judge its precision and comprehensiveness carefully to allow you some flexibility.

Overall a variety of techniques can be used. None may be a magic formula, but together they add substance to how you are able to work. Silence, being prepared to hold on (mentioned earlier), is a good example. There are other such devices.

» *Keeping track*: never lose the thread or your grip on the cumulative details; it helps to summarize regularly and to make notes as the meeting progresses.
» *Being seen to be reasonable*: you can keep the perception of your attitude and of progress to date positive simply by the tone of voice and phrase you adopt: *that's a good point - good idea, let's do that, it should work well*.
» *Reading between the lines*: nothing may be quite what it seems - or sounds - and you need to watch for "danger phrases" from the other side, e.g. *that's everything* (meaning *everything - for now, but there are more demands to come*), *right, that's good all round* (*and especially good for me*).
» *Focusing on the arrangements*: if you want a deal, then you must proceed as if there is potentially one to be had; making it sound as if you may not proceed at all casts doubt on the whole process.
» *Concentrating*: keep thinking and run the conversation to allow this, building in pauses if necessary, e.g. say *Let me think about that* and pause, make a telephone call - whatever. But never be rushed ahead on an ill-considered basis.
» *Considering matters in the round throughout*: be careful not to go for final agreement only to find out that the other party is still introducing new issues; there is a particular danger in agreeing to

parts of the proposition one by one and then finding you are left with nothing to bargain with towards the end.

» *Always regarding timing as a variable*: deadlines, duration and every other aspect of time are almost always negotiable.

» *Always questioning what is described as fixed*: what seem like constraints can often be made into variables and included in the trading.

Any such list (and it could well be extended) quickly makes the point about the juggling trick that negotiating usually presents. The principles are individually straightforward, but there are a fair number of them so the orchestration of the whole process needs skill and benefits from practice. It is important therefore to keep control. Containing emotions if necessary, and certainly remaining neutral, organized, not being rushed and being prepared to question matters as they are introduced, are vital.

Overall you should aim to run the kind of meeting you want, and create one that the other party will see as businesslike and acceptable.

Remember that any confidence and professionalism you project will position you as someone to be respected, and that in turn may prevent certain more outrageous demands even being voiced. For instance, refusing to get hung up on something (even though it is, for you, a key issue), but rather being prepared to bypass it - *to avoid getting bogged down, let's leave that, it's not so important, if we discuss so and so next we can pick it up later* - can impress. And so too can remembering to slot it in later, picking it up at an appropriate point (though the other party may hope it has been forgotten) and dealing with it in a different way to avoid stalemate.

Interpersonal behavior

The thoughts above, keeping control, with emotion under wraps and so on, bring us naturally to the behavioral factors involved. Again there are many, but the following are selected to give a feel of how they affect matters.

» *Disguised motivation*: consider spelling out your true meaning and asking others to do the same. It is possible to have so much double guessing going on - *why are they asking that?* - that no one knows what is happening.

» *Advance warning*: the above can be helped by what many refer to as clear "signposting." This is best done positively - *It might help meet the timing considerations if* . . . - so that it is clear why a suggestion is being made. Negative signs ahead of a counter argument are often just a cue for the other person to stop listening as they begin to marshal their response - *I'm not letting them get away with that, I'll suggest* . . .

» *Tactics to disrupt*: it should be recognized that not only is all fair in love and war, but that negotiating can be regarded as coming into this category also. Some - many - things are done to throw you (and you may want to act similarly). Examples include throwing out a smokescreen of many demands with the intention of getting agreement to one key one hidden amongst others that are, in fact, less important; or the use of flattery or coercion, a (contrived) outburst of anger, disbelief or outrage, pretended misunderstanding, playing for time (or imposing an unrealistic deadline on discussions), and more.

» *Giving nothing away*: meant here in the sense of poker playing impassiveness. If you sound firm, you must look firm - even if you are wondering what on earth you can do next. There is a link here with body language which, while something of an uncertain science, may be worth a thought (or reading up on - see Chapter 8).

On the other hand, rather than disrupting, some points need to be powerfully made and are in the nature of attack. If this is the case then it is important not to allow people to be put on their guard. This may be easily done, perhaps out of sheer politeness, with a circumspect statement like - *look, I'm sorry to insist but this really is something I must handle carefully*. There are things about which we must be much more direct *It is impossible for me to go that far*. Full stop.

Keeping on track

Negotiating is just a special form of communication. So all the rules of good communication apply if negotiation is to be successful, and some of them are key.

Taking the need for clarity as read (if not always faultlessly achieved!), perhaps two are key. They go together and are listening and asking questions.

» *Questioning*: successful negotiators never try to proceed on the basis of hunch or assumption. If something is said that might be ambiguous, then they check it. Whether it is better to do this head on or obliquely is a question for individual circumstances, and both will have their place. But, one way or another, negotiating must proceed on the basis of clear understanding. Ask. Use open questions (i.e. those which cannot be answered "yes" or "no") as these are most often best at obtaining information quickly and precisely. Get people talking. Pursue their real meaning and feelings, if necessary with a series of linked questions, and build what you discover into the plan you have made, adjusting how you implement it and fine-tuning as you go.

» *Listening* is equally important. The great danger is to allow your mind to wander, albeit constructively, as you think ahead, when in fact this is not useful unless you have first picked up every detail and every nuance of what is said. There is no harm in being thought of as someone who misses nothing, whether on or between the lines. People are more careful if they think they are negotiating with someone who is confident and professional. Listening seems obvious, yet needs working at, and because it makes a real difference some consideration of how you can make sure it is effective is worthwhile (see box).

CHECKLIST: ACTIVE LISTENING SKILLS

» *Want to listen*: this is easy once you realize how useful it is to the negotiating process.

» *Look like a good listener*: people will appreciate it and, if they see they have your attention, feedback will be more forth-coming.

» *Understand*: it is not just the words but the meaning that lies behind them you must note.

» *React*: let people see that you have heard, understood and are interested. Nods, small gestures and signs and comments will encourage the other person's confidence and partici-pation – *right?*

» *Stop talking*: other than small acknowledgements, you cannot talk and listen at the same time. Do not interrupt.

» *Use empathy*: put yourself in the other person's shoes and make sure you really appreciate their point of view.

» *Check*: if necessary, ask questions promptly to clarify matters as the conversation proceeds. An understanding based even partly on guesses or assumptions is dangerous. But ask questions diplomatically, do not say *You didn't explain that properly*.

» *Remain unemotional*: too much thinking ahead – however can I overcome that point? – can distract you.

» *Concentrate*: allow nothing to distract you.

» *Look at the other person*: nothing is read more rapidly as disinterest than an inadequate focus of attention - good eye contact is essential; in negotiating, lack of it will always be read as deviousness.

» *Note particularly key points*: edit what you hear so that you can better retain key points manageably.

» *Avoid personalities*: do not let your view of someone as a person distract you from the message, or from dealing with them if that is necessary.

» *Do not lose yourself in subsequent arguments*: some thinking ahead may be useful; too much and you suddenly may find you have missed something.

» *Avoid negatives*: to begin with clear signs of disagreement (even a dismissive look) can make the other person clam up and destroy the dialogue.

» *Make notes*: do not trust your memory, and if it is polite to do so, ask permission before writing their comments down.

As the variables are juggled to and fro, remember that there will be an intention behind everything said and done. If, early on, someone repeatedly says that some element of the discussion is not negotiable it could mean just that. Or it could mean they hope to persuade you not to seek to use it as a variable even in a small way, even though they would be prepared to do so. If so, then a good tactic is to leave it on one side, gain agreement on other issues and establish a rapport before going back to test just how strong the resolve about the "non-negotiable element" is in the face of an attractive agreement developing.

If someone reacts with shock, horror and surprise to a suggestion, you may have genuinely taken them unawares. Just as likely they hope to agree a rapid concession on the back of their exaggerated response. If so, then ignoring the tenure of the first response and asking for a more considered comment may provide a better basis on which to move forward.

Such ploys and responses are the nuts and bolts of negotiating. Their permutations are virtually endless. But whatever form they take, they are better dealt with from the firm foundation of a considered understanding of the negotiating process and how it works. For some people in business, one aspect of the profile of an individual may well be how they are seen as negotiators.

Again this can take many forms. It might be the admin. department, seemingly with no feel for commercial details, securing an especially keen deal with a supplier; the sales person boosting profitability with a keen deal; or it might be an accountant who, impressing a client with the apparently effortless professionalism with which they strike a deal on their behalf and in their presence, raises their profile sufficiently to prompt the client to allow them to act on their behalf again on other issues. In many different circumstances negotiating can achieve a variety of different things – both corporate and personal.

KEY INSIGHTS

The list of techniques reviewed here is many and varied. It is not possible to mention them all again by way of summary, however the key things to remember are that you must:

» *cope with the complexity*: and this means having a sound understanding of how the process works;
» *manage the discussion*: and this means taking time to prepare and keeping a steady hand on the tiller, as it were, throughout the discussion; and
» *focus on the other party throughout*: because everything about what you do needs to be based on as good an understanding of the other party's needs, style and tactics as you can discover (both before and during discussion).

Negotiating, or rather well-handled negotiating, can be very useful. When push comes to shove, a considered and careful – indeed watchful – approach, systematically applied is probably best; and remember the saying attributed to Lord Hore-Belisha: *"When a man tells me he is going to put all his cards on the table, I always look up his sleeve."* This sentiment should be regarded as good advice by any good negotiator.

In Practice

"There are some men – who in a fifty-fifty proposition – insist on getting the hyphen too."

Laurence J. Peter, educationalist and author

"When a person with money meets a person with experience, the person with the experience winds up with the money and the person with the money ends up with the experience."

Harvey Mackay

Negotiating is a process that reflects the style and confidence of the individual. If you are – or can appear – powerful, then you may make a better deal (though pushed too far people may respond by walking away). There are examples of real or apocryphal negotiation that make this point, showing how style affects outcome.

» An actor in negotiating with movie magnate Sam Goldwyn demanded "*$1500 a week.*" "*You're not asking $1500*" growled the movie man "*You're asking $1200 – and I'm giving you $1000.*" *Moral*: status, manner and confidence does make a difference.

» The downfall of United Kingdom Prime Minister, Edward Heath (now Sir Edward Heath) came in negotiating with the striking miners' union in the infamous time of the "three day week." He made an offer and refused to budge. He was simply not believed. The union knew that that was not how negotiating works; there is always some give and take. The result was stalemate and the resignation of a government. *Moral*: the ritual of negotiating needs respecting.

» Complexity may make for long negotiation (the negotiation that ended the Korean War took two years and 575 separate meetings), but too much haste may be worse. George Ball, one of President Kennedy's advisors during the Cuban missile crisis, has spoken of the long discussions that took place at that time. "*Had we determined our course of action within the first 48 hours after the Russian missiles were discovered we would almost certainly have made the wrong decision.*" The implication is that this would have led to war. *Moral*: never be rushed into something unless you are content you have considered it fully and in sufficient detail.

LINKING THEORY AND PRACTICE

Enough has been said in Chapter 6 to demonstrate that negotiating is a practical art. It is one thing to dissect and discuss it, but it is another to put it into practice. So, given the interactive nature of the process, it is appropriate to give reasonable space to examining an example of an actual negotiating meeting in this section.

The case study that follows illustrates a typical negotiating situation within a sales context; it is set out to facilitate an analysis of the detail of what is being done and how well it is working.

The situation

Pat is a freelance journalist, working from home and writing articles, company material and doing some public relations work. With her business growing she has decided to update her computer equipment. Following some research – she has decided what she wants – she arranges for a salesman from a local office equipment company to visit her and discuss his company's quotation.

In the conversation reported, the decision to purchase has been made, provided Pat can get the sort of deal she wants. If not, then she is prepared to talk to another supplier. Below is what each protagonist plans to get from the meeting.

Pat wants to keep costs down

Pat has debated long and hard with herself about what she can afford. It is very important to her to have something good. She wants the larger and faster of the two printers she has checked out. Above all she would like to minimize the cost. Yet by going into the matter she has realized there are additional items such as extra software that could be worth obtaining as well. The specifications in the quote include two additional software packages. Finally, a small point – she is worried about being away from her desk for any training that may be necessary.

John is confident of a sale

John believes he is close to an order. The equipment seems to be exactly what is wanted and he has offered a reasonable deal. He has some leeway on price, either in terms of a reduction or juggling with other elements of the package, but wants a profitable sale. He sees it as the last part of the sales process rather than a negotiation. He is mistaken in this view and therefore not as appropriately prepared as he should be.

Looking out for variables

Various elements are used as variables during the conversation. These include: the equipment itself, the software, delivery and installation, training, payment terms, price and discount and even publicity.

Note: Comments appear in italics periodically about the conversation as it proceeds. There are numbers marking various stages; these link to the checklist shown at the end.

Managing the ebb and flow of the process

John (J) is sitting in Pat's (P) office. The initial pleasantries are over, Sue has organized coffee for them, and John now takes the initiative and turns to the business of the day.

J   You got our quote then?

P   Yes, thanks very much.

J   I hope you found it interesting. *(He tests to discover her initial attitude.)*

P   Yes, indeed. I am not sure it is exactly right and I am comparing it with some others, but it was certainly clear. [1] *(She indicates that she is looking at other quotes and hints that they are also good, perhaps better.)*

J   I see, in what way is ours not quite right? *(Here he attempts to clarify the last comment.)*

P   Technically I am sure it is quite good. I am not a technical person [2], of course, but you seem to have reflected my brief well enough and I have no quibbles with that. However, I am after a total system. Not just the word processor itself, but the software, printer and things like training as well. I think it is these areas we need to have a closer look at. *(She aims to soften John up.)*

J   I see, perhaps you would tell me where you see any particular problem? *(He seeks further clarification.)*

P   *(Pat prefers to deal with one thing at a time and in the sequence of her choice. She starts with the other equipment.)* I think there are several areas. Perhaps we can take them one at a time. Let's deal with the ancillary equipment first. In your quote you recommend the faster of the two laser printers we discussed. As you know I really want the faster printer rather than the more basic one if I can, and both a CD-ROM drive and a DVD one, so I can liaise with a colleague who has material on that system and get myself more up-to-date.

(She indicates the total is too expensive.) Now this will certainly do everything I want, a Rolls Royce job in fact, but that printer does make the whole package more than I really hoped to spend [3]. *(She asks for a concession, trading something of low importance to her: the two drives.)* I am not sure that the second disk drive is essential anyway. I am well able to manage without it. So what I suggest we do is that you let me have the DVD drive on loan long enough to test it out.

J   It is just the additional disk drive that you want on that basis? *(He clarifies.)*

P   Yes. If I do want to keep it then it will postpone the payment for that element for just a while and that means I can go for the better printer. See what I mean? *(This was always her intention.)*

J   Yes, I do.

P   It won't be difficult for you to arrange that [4] I am sure, and if I decide in favor you will get payment for it anyway in, say, six months. *(She minimizes the difficulty the point may make for him.)*

J   Okay, I suppose I can arrange that. I'm pretty sure you will want to keep it anyway. *(He concedes what appears to him a small point.)*

P   *(She confirms the concession and turns to the second point: software ...)* I expect you're right. Good, that's fine. Let's turn now to the question of software. I would ideally like the graphics package, and the one that will do my accounts, as well as the full word processing one. Would you be able to include those at no extra charge? *(She asks for another concession.)* They are not very costly but I must keep the overall cost down, as I've said.

J   You didn't include those in the spec we quoted, or did you? *(He begins to resist.)*

P   No, I'm sorry. I hadn't been through all the literature at the time, but I can see they would be useful. It would make your overall arrangements much more attractive. [5] *(She apologizes but repeats the request.)*

J   It is an extra cost for us, though. *(He continues to resist.)*

P   Not very much in terms of the overall cost. *(She persists, minimizing the effect.)*

J   Well, perhaps not. I guess I could let you have those if we go ahead. *(He agrees, reluctantly, to include the extra software.)*

P   And you will deliver that along with everything else and include a run-down on them in the training? *(She adds a request for a small, related, concession.)*

J   Well I don't know, it will extend the training time and ... *(John realizes he has in fact given away more than he thought.)*

P   But they are not much good unless I can work them. I am sure I will pick it up fast and it won't extend the time to any real extent. *(The point is pressed and the difficulty – time and cost – minimized.)*

J   Alright. *(He agrees.)*

P   I appreciate that. Now, what next? Ah yes, the delivery and installation. *(Pat raises the third point: delivery and installation.)*

J   Well, that should be straightforward. Is that the last point? *(John attempts to get the rest of her shopping list.)*

P   Yes. [6] Well, apart from training but I am sure that's no problem. It's all included and you agreed to run me through the other software. *(She belittles what is described as the last point.)*

J   Yes, okay. What about delivery? Here I suppose? *(Reassured, John goes back to the third point.)*

P   That's right. I've ordered one of those units for it all to stand on. Once I know which quote I accept I can get that and away we go. Your people do install, don't they? I don't want a pile of boxes dumped on the doorstep.

J   Yes, of course. Delivery and installation were all included.

P   And you will take away all the boxes and packing? *(She asks for a small extra.)*

J   We don't usually do that. Can't you leave them for the dustman?

P   The Residents' Association is a bit strict about that sort of thing and the chairman lives next door. In fact, he wants to come and see what equipment I get. If you can get all the boxes taken away I can possibly recommend you. [7] I believe he is thinking of a similar installation for his firm. *(Pat hints at future business prospects as a lever to obtain the concession.)*

J   I'm still not sure that I can arrange that. Our dispatch manager is very strict.

P   See what you can do, will you? *(This point is left hanging but Pat has a nice case to make to whoever delivers – "He said he'd fix it.")*

J   *(He tries to move on to the last point and explains what needs to be done.)* Okay, I will. Now what about training? If you decide to go ahead today, then I can get a date in the diary for you to visit the training center.

P   And you think a day will be enough even with the other software included? *(She checks details.)*

J   Oh yes, certainly. How about the week after next? *(He goes for agreement.)*

P   Hang on, I was hoping you could get your trainer to come here. Would that be possible? *(But Pat introduces another, unexpected concession she wants.)*

J   It is certainly possible, but there would be an extra cost. *(He is determined to give nothing more away.)*

P   You remember I mentioned earlier the other quotes I have? [8]

J   Yes.

P   One of the differences is that they are both willing to do the training here. It means I don't have to leave my phone unattended. That's important to someone working on their own. If we schedule the date well ahead it would minimize the inconvenience. *(Pat aims to make him feel uncompetitive just at a stage when he believes everything is agreed, and minimizes the problem.)*

J   Even so, we have a clear scale of charges for in-house visits and with what I have already agreed . . . *(He resists.)*

P   I see the problem but it would be a pity to fall out at this stage. Everything else seems fine. May I make a suggestion? *(She emphasizes the prospect of the order.)*

J   What, exactly? *(He tries to clarify.)*

P   I have been asked by one of the office equipment journals (she names a well-known one) to write a feature on the writer's use of word processors. If I buy yours I shall have to use it as an example – after all it will be the only one I've got! If I promise to mention your firm by name, do you think your boss would agree to the training being done here? It would be such a help. At least ask him, he might like the idea. [9] *(Pat makes the request seem to have clear compensations. She sells it.)*

J I can certainly ask, it sounds a good swap to me. Will you leave it with me? *(John conditionally agrees.)*

P Yes, of course. See what reaction you get.

J Right. So we seem to be agreed. We let you have the second drive on six months' loan, include the additional software, and I will work on the training being done here.

P And on getting all the boxes cleared away, yes?

J That's right, nearly forgot. Can we go ahead on that basis? *(He tries to wrap up the deal.)*

P Yes, I think we can ... but there is just one small thing. Again this is included in the other quotes. That's insurance. *(Pat raises an extra area.)*

J What do you mean? *(John queries this.)*

P They offer a free year's insurance as part of the package.

J On the same machine and costing?

P Not exactly, I suppose, but similar. *(Pat concedes it is not exactly like for like.)*

J You have to look at the other deal, you know. With the price we have quoted and the extras there is no possibility of my matching that. *(A straight refusal.)*

P *(Pat suggests how reasonable she is ... and raises a price objection.)* Well, I suppose I have to accept that. Even so it is a bit of a disappointment. Your company offers the best arrangements in many ways, but even with the items we have agreed it is still not the most competitive. I take it you do want the business?

J Yes, indeed we do.

P Perhaps you would consider adjusting the overall discount to make up for my having to fix and pay for insurance separately? *(Now she adds a suggestion...)*

J I believe our original price was very keen. We do, as I said, want the order, but I don't really have any more leeway over the discount. *(...which is resisted.)*

P I'm sure your price is keen, but as I said it is not the most competitive. *(Pat puts his quote on the spot by reminding him of the competition.)*

J What sort of difference are we talking about?

P To really make everything we have said add up to the best deal all round, I suppose the discount would need to go up by seven and a half per cent or so.

J That's a lot of money, the margins on this kind of system are not so great. *(He resists.)*

P How far could you go? *(She squeezes.)*

J Myself? I think with what we have already agreed I could not go beyond four per cent at this stage. That would be my limit.

P And how far could your company go at the next stage? [10] *(Pat presses to test that the overall limit is really being reached.)*

J "At this stage" was just a turn of phrase. Four per cent would be the company's limit.

P No good me calling your boss, you mean? *(This comment questions his status and authority.)*

J No, I'm afraid not.

P But you can go to four per cent more discount?

J Yes, I can.

P *(Pat belittles his offer.)* I hoped you would go to seven and a half per cent to match the others completely, but let's see what we have agreed. *(Then recaps and throws in the current price.)* You will lend me the second drive and invoice after six months at the current price, you will include the other software and find out about the training and the boxes and reduce the price by another four per cent.

J Yes, that's it.

P On that basis, I think we have a deal. Would you like another coffee while we tie up the paperwork? *(Pat closes the discussion and has the deal she is going with.)*

Using the dynamics of the meeting

Pat had thought about what she wanted. She had considered the process that was to be involved. She did not expect the meeting to go exactly as planned, but used the changing circumstances to feel her way through it. She had firm objectives, but had to deal with a dynamic situation as the other party, of course, had their own intentions.

There are still loose ends but the deal has improved markedly. It may be that Pat is depicted as doing too well, though no doubt the salesman has still got a profitable deal. She handled it well and deserved to win the majority of points. She certainly did better than others, approaching the same process less well prepared, might have done. We might imagine she did better than John had expected; he perhaps departed the meeting muttering about customers getting more demanding by the day.

Adding up the score

The outcome might be summarized as follows. John gets his order, of course, but Pat wins a number of concessions.

» Six months loan of the DVD disk drive, and later payment for it at current prices.
» Two additional, free, pieces of software.
» The boxes and packing taken away on delivery perhaps.
» Training at her home, rather than at the training center probably. She could have opted to make her order conditional on this.
» An additional four per cent discount.
» She has not managed to get free insurance, and has offered collaboration on an article, and tacitly promised a recommendation to a friend.
» Pat has saved enough to finance the printer she really wanted and still come out ahead. She led the process: she worked through systematically, she was prepared, she negotiated. John, on the other hand, emerges sadder but wiser. He has the order, it may even be reasonably profitable, but he is no doubt saying to himself *if only* ...

Reading the signs

All negotiating will have a sub-text of hidden meaning. Some words disguise the true feeling, some can draw attention to the fact that all is not quite as it seems. The numbers in the preceding text indicate some examples of this, and the things said which are highlighted are related to possible real, underlying meanings shown below.
Text number

   1 ... it was certainly clear. *(But not exactly right.)*
   2 I am not a technical person ... *(You can handle me easily.)*

3 . . . does make the whole package more than I really hoped to spend . . . *(I may not buy from you unless I get a better deal.)*
4 It won't be difficult for you . . . *(A little flattery . . .)*
5 . . . make your overall arrangement much more attractive. *(Without it is less, or not at all, attractive.)*
6 Yes. *(For the moment.)*
7 . . . I can possibly . . . *(Nothing promised, no degree of likelihood.)*
8 Remember . . . the other quotes. *(I am not decided yet – don't lose it at this stage.)*
9 He might like the idea. *(And thank you for it.)*
10 . . . at the next stage. *(Can anyone else in your organization decide differently?)*

Fine tuning your approach

As this example shows, it is from the thinking done prior to the meeting and the plan made that the first direction springs. As the case here shows, negotiating is a dynamic affair. You can never be sure of what will happen. Even quite minor variances from what is expected or planned can necessitate changes to how the meeting is then handled.

Such changes produce opportunities and challenges. The good negotiator is quick on their feet and remains open to fine tuning the approach as the meeting proceeds. It is best to assume this will be necessary. You will not anticipate everything, nor will you spot every opportunity, but neither will your opponent. If you can fine tune in a way that stays a jump ahead, that may be sufficient to get the deal you want.

TEAM NEGOTIATING

The above is a simple example, but also typical – many negotiations do involve just two people. But a team may be involved on either, or both, sides. There are dangers in this approach; a team may fragment and disagree amongst themselves. But a well-organized team has considerable strength. It can share the tasks of planning, listening, watching, talking, and noting and remembering details. Working with others can raise the confidence of all concerned.

Various roles can be defined.

» *Leader*: someone must be in the chair for the team; their role is one of leadership and co-ordination. This does not necessarily mean they must talk first, most or loudest.

» *Reviewer*: has a special focus on summarizing and clarifying; they need to work closely with the leader but not take over their role and introduce new issues (sometimes in long negotiations the reviewer may substitute for the leader in certain sessions).

» *Observer*: a member of the team who is concerned with reading between the lines, trying to watch and ascertain the other side's objectives, priorities, needs and how they are fine tuning their progress and what tactics they are using.

» *Analyst*: or recorder. This person is not just a scribe, though a clear written note may be invaluable, but also concerned to interpret the information (and often, of course, the figures) that are on the table.

Organizing an effective team is an important task. Deciding who will be included and who will not (both to keep numbers manageable and to exclude people who are unsuitable) must be done carefully. Briefing, and sometimes rehearsal even, must be undertaken seriously – and a sufficient time allocated to so doing. This latter point is worth emphasizing. Many such negotiations suffer not because the strategy they adopt or the people involved are inappropriate, but solely because time to plan and prepare was skimped and, on the day, the left hand was not sure what the right hand was supposed to be doing.

A CREATIVE APPROACH

Beyond the essential deployment of the techniques of negotiating there is room for more, for ideas that change – perhaps radically – your position in the negotiating and improve your chances of success. Ideas here can clearly go too far and an element of risk is involved, but it is worth thinking about; the two examples shown illustrate the kind of thing hinted at here.

» It is said that an advertising agency that was negotiating with British Railways about a campaign for the Pullman (refreshment) services on trains kept the BR team waiting a long time in their reception.

The area was noisy and untidy, and after the BR team began to be impatient indifferent tea and coffee were served in paper cups, on a dirty tray swimming in coffee dregs and biscuit crumbs. Finally, just before they walked out, the team were shown into the conference room. As he welcomed them, the agency man explained that they had just seen how their passengers saw the existing service on their trains and that they would help them put this right. A risky strategy no doubt (though reputed to have worked) and – true or not – the story illustrates a creative approach; one can certainly imagine that the agency team would be seen in a good light for their novel approach.

» In a the smart European office of a company making ball bearings a consultant is negotiating with management about a training contract. As he came into reception he was given a visitor's pass, stamped with his name and time of arrival. As he left, the card was replaced with one recording the impressive number of ball bearings made in the factory during the duration of his visit. Rather than keeping it he asked for an envelope and sent it back to the manager in the marketing department with whom he had been in discussions with a copy of his business card attached. On the card he wrote a short phrase: ... *but how many have you sold?* Again there is a risk involved here, the manager might have thought it impolite, but in fact, following a meeting about training, intended to improve sales results, it made the right impression – the terms of the deal were agreed without further discussion.

Both these examples act to change positively the image and therefore, in terms of negotiations, the power of the people concerned. Ideas of this sort can be an important part of establishing the relationship inherent in negotiating and are worth some thought – and some careful judgment.

KEY INSIGHTS

To negotiate successfully you must see the process in the round, take a broad view and continue to do so throughout the process. This means you must have a good grasp of the principles involved, for it is that which allows you the opportunity to orchestrate and fine tune the process as you proceed. Small adjustments as you progress can make all the difference.

We end this section with two checklists designed to encapsulate the essentials that make the process work in practice.

Checklist 1: summarizing the principles

» Definition: negotiating is about bargaining to reach a mutually agreeable outcome. This is the "win-win" concept.

» Never neglect your preparation. Have a clear plan but remain flexible.

» Participants must regard each other as equals. Mutual respect is essential to both conduct and outcome.

» There is a need to abide by the rules. Negotiating is about discussion, rather than debate. There is little place for overt one-upmanship or domination, yet each must fight their corner.

» Put your cards on the table, at least on major issues. Do not pretend powers or state intentions that are untrue.

» Patience is a key characteristic of the good negotiator. Take your time; do not rush discussion or decision making. Delay is better than a poor outcome.

» Empathy is vital. Put yourself in the other's shoes; see things objectively from their point of view.

» State clear objectives. Being open early on about overall intentions can save groping in the dark.

» Avoid confrontation. Do not get into a corner you cannot get out of. Avoid rows and showdowns, but stand firm and keep calm.

» Treat disagreement carefully. Act as devil's advocate, apparently looking at the case from the other's viewpoint, to avoid a "confrontational – I disagree" style.

» Deal with concessions progressively. Where concessions have to be made, make them unwillingly and one at a time – and trade them.

» Do not let perfection be the enemy of the good. An outcome that is one hundred per cent what you want is rarely an option.

Be realistic. Do not waste time and effort seeking something out of reach.

» Use openness but not comprehensively. Declaring your plans and intentions may be useful to the discussion. You may want to keep hidden the motivation behind them.

» Stick with your objectives. Set your sights high and settle as high as possible. Know when to drop the whole thing rather than agree a totally inappropriate deal.

» Keep up your guard. Maintain your stamina, bide your time. The other party may persevere for hours to see when you will crack.

» Remain professional. For example, respect confidences that are given in the course of negotiations. Such consideration builds relationships and may help you next time.

» Never underestimate people. A velvet glove may be disguising an iron fist.

» End positively. Neither party will get exactly what they want, but if the deal is agreeable emphasize this at the end.

Checklist 2: summarizing the tactics

Like any interactive skill negotiating is dependent on a plethora of factors. The following are picked to provide a top ten of things likely to be most useful. You might like to compose your own list, see how it varies and make sure it reflects exactly the kind of negotiating you do and the kind of people it pits you against.

» Select the right starting point. Your plan should make it easy for you to take the initiative and quickly get onto your agenda.

» Aim high, then the trading moves you nearer to what you regard as a good position.

» Do not make your feelings obvious. There is an element of bluff. If your face and body language say *this is minor*, as you respond to something major, you will do better.

» Use silence. Some things demand no reaction at all.

» Watch for early difficulty. Let a rapport and momentum build up before you tackle contentious issues.

» Do not exaggerate facts. They can be verified and exaggeration causes problems later.
» Communicate clearly. Remember the need for understanding as a foundation to the whole process.
» Be seen to go with the other person's way of doing things, at least to some degree and particularly if you are on their ground.
» Do not push too hard. There is usually a line beyond which the outcome is not a better deal, but complete breakdown.
» When negotiating is finished, stop. Once agreement is reached, clear, agreed and perhaps noted, move on to other matters. Otherwise people say *I have been thinking* . . . and you are back to square one.

The importance of different factors like these depends on the nature of the negotiating. Something full of complex financial details poses different problems from something simpler. Finally, a few things to avoid. You will only excel if you never:

» over-react if responses are negative; the other person is at pains not to say how excellent every point is;
» allow yourself to become over-emotional, unpleasant, provocative or insulting; a planned and controlled display of emotion may be useful, but you must know what you are doing; and
» agree to something you do not want; in many situations there is a minimal deal that your plan should identify, below which it is better to walk away.

Every negotiating situation you face can teach you something: what works well, what should be avoided, what best fits your style. The detail is important. Sometimes what makes the difference between success and failure is small and seemingly insignificant. One phrase, even one gesture may make such a difference. If all the details are right, the whole will be more likely to work well.

Key Concepts and Thinkers

"A prudent man must always follow in the footsteps of great men and imitate those who have been outstanding. If his own prowess fails to compare with theirs, at least it has an air of greatness about it."

Niccolo Machiavelli (1469-1527), perhaps the fist seminal influence on negotiating and power politics

"Silence is even better than asking questions if the mood is right; it is always a hard argument to counter. Your opponent will give away his thoughts, approach, opinions, strategy. Talk less; learn more. There is a weight in silence, a great value in an interval in presenting your argument, an influential thoughtfulness in a pause."

Michael Shea, author and former press secretary to Queen Elizabeth II

GLOSSARY

There are certainly a number of technical terms stemming from the negotiating process. Some of these are worth noting and have a precise meaning which is important to the successful practice of negotiating.

Arbitration - This term is usually applied to negotiation designed to settle disputes, especially where negotiations involve a third party and both sides agree to be bound by their, objective, decisions. In the United Kingdom ACAS, The Advisory Conciliation and Arbitration Service, is a national body able to provide help when organizations fall out.

Bargaining - Another word implying negotiating (one which has fewer business connotations and makes the process sound simpler). Essentially it is a euphemism for negotiating, albeit one that implies the least complex end of the scale.

Blocking - A blocking statement is one designed to stop argument and channel discussions in a particular direction; it is a prefix to the point being made.

Body language - The signs given out through someone's stance, behavior and gestures which (with varying degrees of accuracy) can cast some light on the status of a conversation or in this case negotiation.

Bogeys – Factors used with the express purpose of adding weight to what is being said; may or may not be of real significance.

Bridge of rapport – Factors introduced to make discussion easier, to prompt discussion and openness and which also direct the conversation along the right lines, i.e. ones that will help whoever is introducing the bridge.

Collective Agreements (and Bargaining) – A term implying that the agreements made, and thus the negotiating however many people are involved in it, are on behalf of a larger group and that all those in the group will be bound by the agreement made.

Concession – A variable that is conceded as part of the trading process; concessions can vary in significance and may be made to appear more or less significant if it helps the case.

Contract – A contract is a legally binding agreement, which is often one of the end results of a negotiation.

Deadlock – A stage at which no progress towards agreement is being made, but from which progress is still potentially possible (as opposed to stalemate, which is a breakdown without any agreement being made).

Defend/attack spiral – A progressive attack, each stage of which will be resisted and which by definition gives warning of negative responses to come.

Escalation – A technique that involves going back on previous offers and asking for more at a stage where someone's position of power has improved and agreement may likely be forced.

Fall-back position – This is essentially "Plan B"; when aiming as high as you wish will manifestly not work, you may need to settle for something less; the fall-back position defines the starting point for this.

Icebergs – This, as the name implies, indicates something largely hidden. In this case they are the reasons why something is rejected. A superficial reason may be the sign of underlying and more fundamental factors of disagreement that need to be brought out into the open.

Irritators – Words or phrases that add nothing to the negotiator's persuasiveness and are likely to be taken in exactly the opposite way from that stated. Thus saying – *this is fair and reasonable* – just alerts people to the fact that it almost certainly is not, at least as far as they are concerned.

Legitimacy – This term classifies factual evidence used to support a case; it must not just seem factual but must be largely unarguable to warrant the term.

Loss leader – A variable that someone finds unimportant and is prepared to sacrifice (ideally in return for something better); its importance will, nevertheless, be maximized to help make an effective trade.

Must-haves – The reverse of the loss leader, factors that are so important that nothing, or nothing significant, can be given away; a true must-have may well mean that no deal is better than the wrong one.

Neutrality – Operating from a neutral position, not putting all your cards on the table at once and apparently remaining open to a variety of solutions.

Nibbling – The technique of posing last-minute additional requests at a stage where it is judged that agreement will come rather than risk the total deal that is so nearly secured.

Ploy – A tactical move in negotiating usually designed to act negatively and stop something, rather than promote a positive move; hence "spoiling tactics."

Point of balance – The place at the end of all the to-ing and fro-ing where agreement is possible and a package of terms and conditions is acceptable to both parties.

Positional bargaining – The opposite of the "win-win" approach, when both parties push their case in isolation from the other and the likelihood is an entrenched position or, if there is an agreement, then one party is left feeling seriously aggrieved.

Power – Many of the approaches used in negotiating produce power, in other words they make the case being made have more "weight" and be less likely to be resisted.

Precedent – Using examples of past success to demonstrate the potential or likely success of something similar being discussed currently.

Psychological attack – Tactics designed purely to rattle or unnerve someone; usually in themselves of no great import, but made effective because of good timing and the confidence with which they are deployed.

Quick kill – A take it or leave it approach designed to end negotiations almost before they have begun; risks major breakdown when used at an early stage.

Signposting – A general communications term for increasing clarity and understanding by flagging in advance where a line of conversation is going; it can apply to either the content or the nature of what is being said.

Soviet-style negotiating – A "win at all costs" approach; can easily prove self defeating.

Stalemate – An irretrievable breakdown of negotiations with no possibility of further progress; as opposed to a deadlock, which might potentially be broken.

Stance – The point from which a negotiator is operating at any particular moment; hence "initial stance" (the position taken up at the start of a meeting).

Trading – The concept of not giving variables away, but trading or exchanging them in some way (with this goes the idea of maximizing the weight of those given, and minimizing the worth of those accepted).

Threat of punishment – Apparent or actual refusal to agree to some specific element important to the other party, especially where this can be done from a position of power and the (seeming) ability to make it stick.

Variable – The elements or individual terms and conditions that negotiating aims to arrange and agree a basis for; these are the basis of the concept of trading and of making, or winning, concessions.

Zone of agreement – The range within which an agreement is possible; an initial stance may be outside this, but final discussions must settle in this bargaining range (this concept was originated by Howard Raffa in *The Art and Science of Negotiating* [Bellnap Press at Harvard University]).

KEY CONCEPTS AND THINKERS

As with any core business skill, especially one that is so extensively documented, there are a great many approaches suggested. Most are useful and essentially only represent slightly different ways of analyzing, thinking about, and deploying the techniques involved in the negotiating process.

Some writers have become regarded as the negotiating gurus. Such include Chester L. Karras, who first wrote on the subject in 1974 (*Give and take*, Thomas Y. Crowell), and went on to spend many years presenting seminars and writing further books and articles. Others of note are G.I. Nierenberg, Herb Cohen and Gavin Kennedy. The last is a Professor at Edinburgh University; he coined the expression "purple" negotiating (a blend of the "red" style of tough tactics and the more sensitive "blue" style of the "win-win" approach. This – which he encapsulates in terms of prepare, debate, propose and bargain stages – makes for a good explanation of the more behavioral side of negotiating (see Chapter 9).

For example, a detailed book like *Cross Cultural Business Negotiations* (see Chapter 9 for details of this and other titles mentioned) sets out early on to define the process in manageable form. It postulates eleven stages:

1. initial planning and fact finding
2. orientation at the site prior to the negotiations
3. non-task (establishing relationships)
4. task-related exchange of information
5. resistance (and overcoming objections)
6. reformulation of strategies (fine tuning the way ahead in light of feedback)
7. hard bargaining and decision making
8. persuasion
9. concessions (and trading)
10. agreement (and setting out and confirming details)
11. follow up.

Alternatively, much shorter encapsulations are favored by some. For example:

1. compromise
2. bargaining
3. threat
4. emotion
5. logical reasoning.

(this is from *Business Negotiating*) and the following, from *Negotiating to Succeed*:

1 prepare
2 discuss
3 propose
4 bargain
5 agreement.

The key stages can perhaps be summarized thus:

» *preparation*: setting ideal/realistic/acceptable terms – anticipate likely responses – create a plan and a strategy;
» *invitation*: move from selling to negotiating – be sure there is agreement to the process – position yourself or your team, i.e. establish their profile;
» *presentation*: set out your ideal terms – ask questions and prompt responses – create, use and build on a relationship;
» *bargaining*: manage the discussions – trade the variables, maximizing and minimizing the value of the variables as appropriate – overcome objections and difficulties; and
» *close*: summarize and clarify the agreement – link to formalization, contractual terms and future dealings – see to any necessary written confirmations after the meeting.

Such checklist style approaches are legion amongst the literature. I will add just one more partly to show the value of training material (where would any trainer be without a few acronyms?) and partly to focus on a key part of the negotiating process, that of trading concessions. The following is an apt reminder of the way such trading must be conducted: ENHANCE and REDUCE:

E - imply that something is EXCEPTIONAL;
N - refer to a NEED that you are satisfying;
H - refer to any previous HISTORY between you;
A - imply that you might be exceeding your AUTHORITY;
N - offer your concession as NOURISHMENT to the relationship;
C - stress the COST to you of the concession;
E - provide EVIDENCE to build up the value of your concession.

Conversely:

R - REDUCE their concession by the way you speak of it;
E - treat it as EXPECTED and take it for granted;
D - DENY it having any real value;
U - UNDERPLAY thanks in both words and tone of voice;
C - CONTRIBUTE it back to them;
E - use EMPATHY *(I can see you might think that would help, but . . .)*.

Certain specific terminology that defines or suggests approaches can be taken from the literature. Examples are given in the following sections.

BATNA

This, coined by Harvard professors Roger Fisher and William Ury, is an acronym for the *Best Alternative To A Negotiated Agreement*. It provides a standard – of no agreement – against which to judge any proposed agreement. It is arrived at in three stages.

1 You list all the alternative actions you might take if there was no agreement.
2 You analyze the list, identify the best and try to improve them.
3 You choose the best possible option – the BATNA.

The idea is that with a BATNA in mind the position from which you negotiate is improved and given power. If you can form a view of what your opponent's BATNA is, this helps too. You can then measure your proposals against realistic alternatives rather than inflexible bottom-line positions.

RESPECT

This acronym, originated by New Zealander Harry A. Mills, divides the approach to negotiating into seven stages.

1 *Ready* yourself (preparation – *"An objective without a plan is a dream,"* Douglas McGregor).
2 *Explore* each party's needs (starting by testing assumptions, asking questions and communicating your opening position).
3 *Signal* for movement (moving to a to and fro process).
4 *Probe* with proposals (making proposals and rearranging rejected proposals).

5 *Exchange* concessions (the trading process).
6 *Close* the deal (making an acceptable and credible deal).
7 *Tie-up* loose ends (confirmations and summary of a complex process).

The stated intention here is to make an agreement that works and lasts, leaving both parties satisfied.

Principled negotiating

This is an approach that goes through four stages.

1 *Separate the people from the problem*: avoiding personalities and emotions (or flagging them openly), understanding the other's point of view, and ensuring every aspect of clear communications.
2 *Focus on interests, not positions*: here the distinction is that position is something decided upon, whereas interests influence the position adopted.
3 *Invent options for mutual gain*: usually defined as searching for a larger cake, rather than arguing over the size of slices.
4 *Insist on objective criteria*: this focuses discussion on criteria independent of people's (perhaps stubbornly) held positions and promotes a "win-win" outcome.

Cultural differences

A number of people have cast light on working across different cultures.

» *Edward Hall*: who suggested basing analysis on two different polarities: high context/low context (that is respectively where discussions tend to be subtle and oblique) and monochromic/polychromic (following an organized basis or a less disciplined approach).
» *Frons Trompenaars*: who based his categorizations on the answers to what are essentially ethical dichotomies such as *Should you run personal errands for your manager?* (China - yes; Australia - no).

Such devices are only useful after you have studied the basis used and have this firmly in mind. Most people want to think about how to deal with one nationality (or a few nationalities) and can take a strictly pragmatic view of the characteristics they have that will need to be born in mind during negotiations. Labeling them (linear-active, high power-distance) and using other terms beloved of the psychologists may not help make tomorrow's meeting go better.

A useful model illustrating those factors that affect negotiating style is used in *Business Negotiating: a Practical Workbook* (Fig. 8.1)

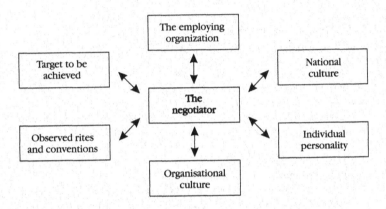

Fig. 8.1 Factors affecting negotiating style.

Body language

Allan Pease is the king of body language. Although some people would question the scientific basis for body language, and it is sensible to regard what it has to say as an indication rather than a certainty, it is a subject the aspiring negotiator might well decide to take an interest in. Probably Australian Allan Pease was the first person to bring it to the attention of people in practical form, and his book *Body Language – how to read other's thoughts by their gestures* (a Sheldon Press paperback) now in its umpteenth edition still makes an excellent and accessible reference.

The boxed paragraph summarizes some of what are regarded as key behavioral signs.

BODY LANGUAGE: SUMMARY OF KEY SIGNS:

Open-mindedness may be shown by:

» open hands
» unbuttoned coat.

Wariness may be shown by:

» arms crossed on chest
» legs over chair arm while seated
» sitting in reversed armless chair
» crossing legs
» fist-like gestures
» pointing index finger
» karate chops.

Thinking/analyzing may be shown by:

» hand to face gestures
» head tilted
» stroking chin
» peering over glasses
» taking glasses off, cleaning them
» earpiece of glasses in mouth
» pipe-smoker gestures
» getting up from table, walking around
» putting hand to bridge of nose.

Confidence may be shown by:

» steepling of the hands
» hands on back of head, authority position
» back stiffened
» hands in coat pockets, with thumbs outside
» hands on lapels of coat.

Territorial dominance may be shown by:

» feet on desk
» feet on chair
» leaning against/touching object
» placing object in a desired space

» hands behind head, leaning back.

Nervousness may be shown by:

» clearing throat
» whew sound
» whistling
» cigarette-smoking
» picking/pinching flesh
» fidgeting in chair
» hands covering mouth while speaking
» not looking at the other person
» tugging at trousers or skirt while seated
» jingling money in pockets
» tugging at ear
» perspiration/wringing of hands.

Frustration may be shown by:

» taking short breaths
» making tutting sound
» tightly clenched hands
» wringing hands
» fist-like gestures
» pointing index finger
» running hand through hair
» rubbing back of neck.

Boredom may be shown by:

» doodling
» drumming fingers
» legs crossed, foot kicking
» head in palms of hands
» blank stare.

Acceptance may be shown by:

» hand to chest
» open arms and hands

» touching gestures
» moving closer to another
» preening.

Expectancy may be shown by:

» rubbing palms
» jingling money
» crossed fingers
» moving closer.

Suspicion may be shown by:

» not looking at you
» arms crossed
» moving away from you
» silhouette body towards you
» sideways glance
» touching/rubbing nose
» rubbing eye(s)
» buttoning coat
» drawing away.

Alertness/attention may be shown by:

» hands on hips
» hands on mid-thigh when seated
» sitting on edge of chair
» arms spread, gripping edge of table.

Keeping in context

The reason for being sensitive to what is said, nuances, gestures, etc. is to help stay in line with the two basic factors of negotiating, your:

» plan
» reading of how things are going and being received.

Such signs should be *not* be taken as a guarantee of particular behavior (a point reinforced when I wrote this on the hottest day of the year, and was conscious that several of my own gestures were no more than a symptom of the heat).

Legal matters

It would be wrong not to mention legal aspects of negotiating. One aspect of a successfully concluded negotiation is often a contract. This may be straightforward – another overseas distributor contract, for instance. Or it may be complicated, as for a company merger. In either case you may need legal advice.

This is not the place to discuss relationships with lawyers, though if they are part of your negotiating team then you certainly need to consider this aspect in appointing them, and to brief them adequately as with any team member. What is worth comment here, with the concentration on negotiating techniques, is how you introduce legal and contractual issues into a discussion, bearing in mind that they can be daunting and off-putting. If such issues are important to you, the boxed paragraph below looks at the implications; it does not assume great complexity, but such things are even more important where this is the case.

CONTRACTUAL ISSUES

The intention of a contract is protective. It secures against what might happen if agreement is not implemented. Sometimes the penalty is considerable; if terms and conditions are not met a significant amount of money may be lost.

For example, if you book a wedding reception, then the bride and groom fall out and there is no wedding, there may still be a large bill to pay. The venue owners, unable to resell the facility at short notice, protect themselves against loss of income by specifying contractual terms.

Making contracts acceptable

For a contractual situation to be acceptable, and not seen as inappropriate, draconian or otherwise unsuitable, certain factors are important. If you are introducing it, make sure that what you do:

» is communicated clearly with no possibility of misunderstandings;

» enhances the relationship involved, if necessary on a continuing basis;
» allows the progressing and securing of agreement to proceed effectively and promptly;
» still allows any necessary flexibility within the arrangement; and
» links logically and neatly to the practicalities involved.

Setting policy

In an organization of any size the first question may be who makes policy decisions and with whom they consult? If you are in charge of such matters, fine; if not you may still have an input to make. Look out for any circumstances not covered by existing policy and be ready to feed back information that may prompt policy change or update.

An example is the wedding reception referred to above. It may be decided that stricter terms and conditions, and penalties for cancellation, are necessary at certain times of year. A wedding function lost in, say, July is perhaps more damaging than at other times as this is peak season.

Addressing the essentials

Contractual arrangements need to make clear:

» the basis of the agreement;
» the terminology to be used by both parties (e.g. is postponement different from cancellation?);
» all elements of timing;
» the procedures, documentation and administration involved; and
» all financial matters in detail.

Introducing contractual matters

A contract may cause problems if it also causes surprise. Produce a ten-page document for signature after hours of debate and discussion that contained no mention of the need for it, and people will twitch. Make matters clear from the beginning.

» Do not apologize for the arrangement, though you may need to explain its necessity.

» Stress the mutual advantages.
» Use language that stresses the joint benefits of clarity, e.g. talk about working together.
» Plan to mention the contractual side progressively, sufficiently early, and set the scene for any detailed discussion about it that may be necessary later.
» Use a checklist to ensure no detail is missed. Make sure all necessary information is to hand, or secured and recorded if it is to be part of the agreement.

The process is progressive and dealing with it may well be spread throughout the meeting.

Dealing with contractual matters

This is often a crucial element of many negotiating discussions. A systematic approach to handling it may therefore be useful.

The following ten key points will help you plan and implement this aspect into the whole of the proceedings.

1 *Introduce the concept of contract.* This needs to be carefully timed. The right moment may pass, and it then gets more difficult to say: *we must have this in writing.* Waiting for the other party to raise things may not be best; you have to plan and be prepared to move the conversation onto the matter. A first mention may simply aim to gain agreement on the need for discussion on it. It may also decide how and when in the discussion this will be done.

2 *Make sure details are clear.* This is an area for crystal clear communication. Different interpretations of one word – *when does provisional become permanent?* may cause disproportionately great problems later.

3 *Make figures and timing especially clear.* Both these are worth being really pedantic about. When, exactly, is the end of the month or year? Again, misunderstanding of such a detail can cause real problems.

4 *Check understanding.* This may be as simple as just saying – *Is that clear* – occasionally, but it is very important. Do not just

think matters are clearly understood between you. You need to know.

5 *Document your side of arrangements*. Make things clear, agree them, then say how you will confirm it and do just that. Delays can cause confusion. It may also help precision of agreement if you take the initiative: write in detail, then they can simply say they agree. Sometimes you may want to do this the other way round to save you time, in discussion with a supplier for example, but read the small print carefully.

6 *Ask for their confirmation*. Do not assume this will come: ask. Chase it if necessary. If contractual arrangements are understood and agreed, you do not have to be circumspect about this.

7 *Chase for action*. This is crucial. If people ignore some key stage, do not feel awkward about reminding them. Make sure you do not forget, put a note in the diary if matters stretch over some time. Delay might well be in the other party's interest.

8 *Adopt the right manner*. Always take a positive approach to contractual matters, stressing that they are important and help both parties. Deal with them in a way that appears efficient, professional and will achieve what you want in the smoothest possible way.

9 *Link to the future*. An agreement and contract made today set the scene for the future. You may want to begin to touch on future arrangements as you tie down a current one. This can pay dividends in the long run.

Being on the receiving end

You will not always be the one introducing contractual matters, of course. When such things are put to you the rules are straightforward.

» Listen, read and check everything that is put over, to make sure you truly understand.

» Take time, if necessary, to consider or to confer with someone else including, if appropriate, a legal mind.

» Be absolutely sure that you can live with the implications, including those of the worst case scenario, before you sign anything.

Tackling breakdown

If you deal with contractual matters in the right kind of way there should be minimal problems. But what if something contractual is agreed and then the other party fails to comply in some way? There are three options.

» *Applying the letter of the law*
The first option is simply to stick to the terms exactly. That is what they are there for. They were agreed. There is no need to feel bad about invoking the conditions. Sometimes this approach will go unchallenged and cause no problems. If not, or if you are yourself worried about souring future arrangements, you may need to take other action.

» *Negotiating a compromise*
Second, if you feel so inclined, you can insist on less than the full terms. You may make some other arrangement that will foster goodwill without your losing anything significant. If the situation is reversed, you may want to insist this is done, to minimize damage to yourself.

» *Making an exception*
This third option is really a variant of the compromise above. It may be important to make it clear that what is done is an exception setting no precedents for the future. If this point is strongly made it may be felt that you are being very reasonable, and this may lead to return compromise in future.

The trick here is to balance avoiding immediate losses with advantages of a more long-term nature. A checklist completes comment on this aspect of negotiating.

Contractual issues checklist

1 Decide appropriate policy and introduce contractual matters into any meeting in a way that sets the scene for what you want to do.

2 Be sensitive to the details involved and ensure mutual understanding of the full picture.

3 Adopt a systematic approach to the way contractual matters are integrated into the discussion.

4 Check and check again before you sign anything.

5 Balance advantages/disadvantages in terms of the severity with which you apply the letter of the law, if this proves necessary.

Numeracy and finance

Though it takes us into a whole different area and the details go beyond our brief here (see, for interest, the *Express-Exec* titles on finance, series numbers 05.01–05.10), this deserves a brief mention. Certainly the importance of suitable competence in this area is vital. You do not only need to understand the financial ramifications of your negotiations; you need to be quick on your feet in juggling with them with someone else who is no doubt eager to maximize financial benefit on their side.

One example of the sort of thing that is important (and for some confusing) will suffice. Consider the question of price negotiations, and just a few representative figures. We need to start with a margin, so assume you operate on a margin of 40%. Then imagine that you are asked for a 15% discount. That does not sound so much – but, to maintain the return demands a 36% rise in turnover! Furthermore, depending on the unit price and quantity sold, quantity sold may have to rise by a still higher percentage to maintain the desired situation. The point is that such figures can surprise. You need an easy familiarity with figures to manipulate them as necessary within your negotiating situations.

Personal characteristics of the good negotiator

Many authors and commentators have their ideas about this; most useful in my view is that of Michael Shea (author of a number of books including *Influence* [Sphere] in which his ideas appear). Briefly paraphrasing him, he believes any good negotiator will:

1 know how to read and assess their opponents (in terms of their needs, plans etc.);

2 know how to assess the strengths and weaknesses the first assessment implies (and also which people in a team are key players and in what role);

3 know how to maximize and minimize aspects of the case as appropriate;

4 be a master at timing, judging accurately when to reveal, or not, their views;

5 be confident in using silence and prompting the other person to say, and reveal, more;

6 have a straight face and an ability to bluff;

7 be able to use the threat of breakdown effectively (and not to overuse it);

8 know how to distract, back off or put the pressure on when appropriate;

9 be effective at applying psychological pressure; and

10 constantly question their opponent's position, especially when under threat.

These ten factors make another good way of summarizing the key issues of this multi-faceted process.

KEY INSIGHTS

In looking for ways to define and specify the techniques of negotiating, it is important to divide information into two parts.

» First, there is a body of techniques which, while variously described in different places and by different authorities, reflects similar core principles; these you need to accommodate, doing so in whatever way you find most manageable.

» Second, there is a plethora of other information to consider. Some of this concerns specific related issues like the skills of persuasion or selling, which are really essential tools to use alongside negotiating. Others are sub-issues, for example body language, and others link to general communications and behavioral issues in terms of how people deal with people.

Overall remember the essentially practical nature of negotiating. Of course it helps to have a clear vision of how it works and a battery of techniques to deploy in your meetings, but negotiating excellence is, as much as anything, a matter of practice. You need to do it, and learn from your experience; though it can also be invaluable to play a part in team negotiating and see and learn from experiencing how other, more experienced people go about it.

Resources

"It is a crunch moment when you are in negotiations. You suddenly see an opening in the hedge and dive through it even if you get scratched."

Len Murray, former general secretary TUC

This section links to the last and is concerned primarily to point out sources of further information, and also what areas of further information might be useful to anyone reviewing the topic of negotiating. A number of disparate topics are reviewed, and we start by returning to the cultural differences mentioned in Chapter 5 The Global Dimension.

CULTURAL DIFFERENCES

There is no substitute for experience relayed straight from the horse's mouth. So faced with negotiating with a Frenchman or Korean for the first time, try to find and chat to someone who has experience of the people and places involved. This need not be someone you know (I remember chatting to someone at the London Chamber of Commerce about my first visit to South East Asia and finding it immensely useful). Beyond that the quickest checks are something like Richard D. Lewis's book *When Cultures Collide* (Nicholas Brealey Publishing), which has excellent introductory chapters before giving a territory by territory account of specific differences.

» Germans and Japanese will ask the difficult questions without preamble.
» The Spaniards will not study the details, but will study you.
» Finns and Swedes will expect you to be up to date (latest computers etc.) like themselves; otherwise you will lack credibility.
» Brazilians, and they are not alone, will never take your first price as the real one and expect it to reduce as discussions continue.

Snippets like the above lead into detailed gameplans for dealing with a whole range of potentially different negotiators.

Or, for really bite-sized comment try Management Pocketbooks: *The Cross-Cultural Business Pocketbook* by John Mattock, and *The Cultural Gaffs Pocketbook* by Angelena Boden. The former contains a succinct description of John Mattock's matrix model enabling a measurement of cultural difference to be made; this was mentioned earlier in Chapter 5. Certainly some research in this area makes good sense.

TRAINING FILMS

These can be an excellent way to get to grips with business skills and techniques of all sorts. They allow you to take in an overview, usually one at pains to encapsulate the key approaches, in a short time. They can be as useful to the individual as to a group or team, and do not necessarily have to be seen within a training context (though of course this may be useful). Usually films, which can be bought or hired (or just taken in at one of the many preview showings which training film producers put on), come with written back-up and the guide or workbook adds to the experience in a palatable way. There is a profusion of material available from around the world (mainly from Britain, America and Australia); two of the best are:

» *Negotiating: tying the knot*: this a provides a clear introduction and overview using an entirely artificial situation (boy meets girl and discuss - negotiate - their future) with a "moderator" articulating and summarizing the key lessons; and
» *Negotiating Profitable Sales*: this is more complex and is in a two-part/two film set; one film deals with preparing to negotiate, the other with conducting the meeting - a more complex industrial example (the sale of construction equipment) allows for more detail to be explored.

Both are useful and both are from Video Arts (who are at Dunbarton House, 68 Oxford Street, London W1N 9LA, UK. Telephone: +44 (0)207-637-7288).

BOOKS

This is an area where there is a profusion of books (and here is another!). Many are in no way novel, while they may provide a good run down on the techniques involved. Some of the best are:

» *Getting to Yes* (Century Hutchinson) by Roger Fisher and William Ury - a readable book that is an excellent introduction and which focuses on interests not positions; and

» *Everything is Negotiable* (Arrow Books) by Gavin Kennedy; a well respected authority in this area gives a good telling of the difficulties and how to overcome them.

As a manageable guide to the essential techniques presented in a particularly accessible form, perhaps I may recommend my own Management Pocketbook - *The Negotiator's Pocketbook* - as a useful presentation of core principles and practices.

A selection of other books includes:

» *New Negotiating Edge: the behavioral approach for results and relationships*, Gavin Kennedy (Nicholas Brealey Publishing);

» *Sales Strategies: negotiating and winning corporate deals*, Chris Newby (Kogan Page);

» *Negotiating the Better Deal*, Peter Fleming (International Thomson);

» *Negotiating Training through Gaming: strategies, tactics and maneuvers*, E.M. Christopher and L.E. Smith (Kogan Page);

» *Instant Negotiating*, B. Clegg (Kogan Page);

» *Negotiating: skills and strategies*, A. Fowler (Institute of Personnel Management);

» *Cross Cultural Business Negotiating*, D.W. Hendon and R.A. Hendon and P. Herbig (Quorum Books);

» *Negotiating to Succeed*, J. Lewthwaite (Hawksmere);

» *Management and Organizational Behavior*, L.J. Mullins (Pitman Publishing);

» *Business Negotiating - A practical workbook*, T. Beasor and P.T. Steele (Gower Publishing);

» *The Complete Negotiator*, G.I. Nierenberg (Nierenberg and Zeif).

In addition, many books on management, marketing, sales, communications, and personnel touch on negotiating. Reading about it is no problem; for those wanting a starting point, the first titles listed may suit, but as much as anything it is a matter of choice (e.g. what do you find readable, do you want a focus on sales?).

JOURNALS

Management and marketing journals seem to touch on the topic of negotiating regularly. So too do journals concerned with purchasing (e.g. *Supply Management*) – indeed it may be useful for those who use negotiating in selling to keep an eye on comment from the buying side (and vice versa).

Some of these reinforce the basic techniques, while others are more academic and focus on complex behavioral issues. Recent examples and their titles show the emphasis:

» Negotiating the "psychological contract" (*Training Journal*, August 2000);
» Breakthrough bargaining: the dynamics of the "shadow negotiating (*Harvard Business Review*, February 2001);
» Contractual aspects of cross-cultural negotiations (*Marketing Intelligence and Planning*, 1997); and
» Neglected phase of the process: contract renegotiating (*International Trade Forum*, 1999).

A PLETHORA OF TECHNIQUES

One of the most useful resources ever published is a ring binder titled *The Negotiator's Tactic Bank*. This is published by the quaintly named Big Sur Publishing and is a compendium of over 200 all-time practical and powerful negotiating tactics. There are a number of sections that take you through every stage of the negotiating process: from "Opening shots" to "Asking the right questions," "Traps and how to avoid them" and "Gaining the upper hand" with each illustrated by a selection of tried and tested approaches. All are set out in a similar format and all are intended to provide a quick checklist-style reference for the negotiator doing their homework and planning their strategy. Written by a panel of experts, the binder makes an excellent companion to any book reviewing the techniques in more conventional form.

We finish this section by reproducing one tactic from this publication to illustrate the style and format involved. See box.

TACTIC 185: ESTABLISHING RAPPORT AT A STICKY MOMENT

"... so, let's make fresh start ..."

No negotiating is likely to be entirely plain sailing for you. You can plan (indeed you should). You can proceed carefully, fine-tuning as you go, but sometimes you hit a crisis. Sometimes it is like when you knock a pile of papers off your desk. Even though you see it coming, you know as you do so that it is too late and then the papers are all over the floor. So, too, with sticky moments in a negotiating meeting; regardless of what has been going on, you are suddenly aware that the agreement is unravelling in your hands, and your carefully planned strategy hits a crisis.

Making the most of a crisis

The cause of the crisis may be either anticipated, that is something you thought might cause problems or a total surprise – perhaps something you could never have anticipated. Whatever the cause, let us assume that a bad initial reaction – because you are thrown – makes things worse. What do you do?

In Chinese, the word crisis is written as two characters: the first is that for the word "chaos," the second is that for "opportunity" – interesting thought. The job here is not just to recover and do so without digging the hole deeper, it is to recover and restart, with the initiative.

The way it works

Mark Hunt is doing well. He is setting up an arrangement with a new distributor for South East Asia. He is sitting with them in an outdoor restaurant attached to his hotel in Singapore and, although there has been a good deal of to-ing and fro-ing, everything seems to be coming together well. He ticks off "initial supply of samples" on his list and is contemplating only a handful of minor matters, so is surprised when Brian Lim says: *"Shouldn't we get back to finalizing a start date? Nothing can proceed without that."* Surprised, his reply is rather abrupt: *"But I thought we had done that – we instigate everything from the start of next year, surely you don't want to go back into all that?"*

His colleague to be is now edgy as well. *"We must,"* he says *"after all . . ."* Mark interrupts: *"But you agreed"* he says *"now you're completely ignoring that fact."* He sees from the expression on Brian Lim's face that his abrupt manner and annoyance is being taken as an insult. *"You asked for the samples to come a month later,"* Brian continues, *"that takes us up against Chinese New Year which, in case you don't realize, disrupts things here for some ten days."*

Mark realizes his mistake. Logically the first delay put back the start date and there is obviously no point in launching so close to a major public holiday.

It's my fault

This sticky moment is his own fault (he had simply forgotten how the one change affected another point *and* was showing his ignorance about local conditions). What does he do next?

Well, the need is to restart. In this kind of situation, ploughing on and trying to adjust matters may not be sufficient to instigate the change that is necessary. A new start is often best made by taking a step back, and finding a sure foothold on a solid foundation of understanding and agreement from which to restart.

The "butterfingers" approach

Mark adopts what might be called the "butterfingers" approach. He apologizes . He admits his mistake. He reassures. And he makes light of his own error – while labeling it (perhaps more acceptably) as a moment of lost concentration. *'Goodness, of course you're absolutely right. My fault, how could I possible forget that changing the sample delivery date will inevitably delay the launch date – I'm sorry, I thought I was over the jet lag! And I had no intention of suggesting that you were neglecting our agreement. Now, we have agreed so much – it's going to be a great opportunity for us both, I'm sure, but it is complicated. Let me recap just a little, then as you say, let's get a launch date that's right for us both absolutely clear before we move on."*

He can now proceed and no damage should be done to either the relationship or the agreements. Of course, sticky moments can occur for all sorts of reasons, and that fault may lie with you, the other person or just with circumstances. So, you do not always need to start with an apology as Mark did here, but otherwise a similar restart makes good sense.

Checklist for getting it right

» Do not plough on and risk digging the hole deeper.
» Flag that a restart is necessary.
» Apologize for any mistake on your part, if necessary.
» Mention good things (linked perhaps to the stage that has been reached).
» Move forward again from an agreed firm foundation, leaving the "stickiness" on one side.

Big Sur Publishing can be contacted at 212 Piccadilly, London W1V 9LD, UK.

KEY INSIGHTS

Just one final thought: the complexities of negotiating are such that *training* may make sense for many people. There is a wealth of courses available from the usual sources, both management and marketing institutes and commercial operators. Choose carefully, and ask for a discount!

Ten Steps to Making Negotiating Work

» Preparation
» Communicate clearly
» Look the part
» Respect the people
» Aim high
» Get their shopping list
» Keep searching for variables
» Utilize the techniques
» Manage and control the process
» Be ever on your guard
» In the beginning

"Hey boys, I've got thousands of jobs at 17 bucks an hour. I've got none at 20. So you better come to your senses."

Lee Iacocca, Chairman Chrysler Corporation

As much of the rest of this work has shown, negotiating effectively needs the understanding and deployment of a range of techniques. Further, much of what makes it successful is in the details and in the sensitivity with which the process is approached. Given the dynamic nature of this interactive skill, it is impossible to restrict comment to ten areas as if they are all that matters, but this is not the intention.

So, here we review ten key areas, some of them leading inevitably to others, which, while not together forming a panacea, help highlight key issues and together summarize something of the nature of the process and its tactics. The first is not only important but there is logic in putting it first.

1. PREPARATION

With a process of the complexity of negotiating, it is not surprising that preparation is key. Early on it accelerates the value of experience, and beyond that it acts to create a valuable foundation to the actual negotiating that follows. In one sense, preparation is no more than respect for the old premise that it is best to open your mind before you open your mouth.

Thus, preparation may consist of a few quiet minutes just before you step into a meeting. Alternatively it may consist of sitting down for a couple of hours with colleagues to thrash out the best tactics to adopt; and everything in between. It can be stretched to include rehearsal, a meeting to actually run through what you want to happen, rather as you would rehearse an important presentation. So:

» give preparation adequate time (and in a hectic life that also means starting far enough in advance);
» involve the right people (because they will be involved in the meeting, or just because they can help); and
» assemble and analyze the necessary information (and take key facts to the meeting).

Preparation should not assume you can then ensure that everything will proceed exactly as planned; planning is as much to help fine tune what is being done when circumstances do take an unforeseen turn. Experience may reduce the time preparation takes; it does not however negate it. Remember too the saying attributed to a famous golfer: *"The more that I practice my game, the more good luck I seem to have."* Never reject preparation as unnecessary, never skimp it in terms of time and effort. It is too late when you come out of a meeting that has not gone well saying - *if only I had*.

2. COMMUNICATE CLEARLY

Like preparation the best way to describe this is as a foundation for success. Your communications within a complex negotiating situation need to be absolutely clear. There is a power that flows directly from sheer clarity and good description. People:

» *understand*: this speaks for itself, but it also means misunderstandings are avoided and it helps ensure that the meeting stays tightly on its real agenda; and
» *are impressed*: clarity gives favorable impressions of authority, certainty and confidence - all of which add to the power you bring to the table.

In addition, clarity about the meeting itself - setting a clear agenda and so on - directs the proceedings and helps make it possible for you to take a lead, which in turn helps get you where you want to go.

Clarity stems from preparation, clear thinking and analysis; and from experience. It is worth working at. The last thing you want at the end of the day is to achieve agreement, only to find it retracted later because someone says that *they were not clear what it was they were agreeing to*. Insisting at that stage can mean you are never trusted again; it is a position to avoid.

3. LOOK THE PART

This may seem obvious but it can have a considerable effect on the outcome of negotiating. A sensible view of the literal aspect of this is clearly prudent; you need to be "smartly turned out" and that needs to be interpreted in light of the circumstances. For example, for a man it might mean a business suit in many contexts, something less formal on occasion and a shirt and tie in a country with a hot climate. Women have more choices to make but the principles to apply are similar.

More important is that certain details give specific impressions, for instance if you are seen as:

» *well prepared*, then people give what you say greater weight;
» *well organized*; it has a similar effect;
» *confident*; this can have a major impact on the credibility of what you say, especially the belief in your insistence that you *can do no more*; and
» *professional*; again a whole raft of characteristics may contribute to this, from being experienced, expert or approachable to something like just appearing not to be rushed and again the case you make will engender more consideration if the person making it is seen in the right light.

The point here is that something can be done to make any such characteristic more visible where this might help, and sometimes this might become a useful exaggeration. Of course what is said is important, but much judgment comes from visual signals and it is wise therefore to use them.

4. RESPECT THE PEOPLE

Negotiating is a cut and thrust process. It *has* an adversarial aspect to it and everyone involved is very much aware of this. While it may be important to take a tough line, to be firm and to insist, this is always more acceptable if the overall tenure of a meeting is kept essentially courteous.

Show that you understand other people's point of view. Be seen to find out what it is, to note details that are important to them and to refer to this during the meeting. Be prepared to apologize, to flatter, to ask opinion and to show respect (in some cases perhaps, whether you feel it is deserved or not!).

Apart from wanting to maintain normal courtesies in what can sometimes be a difficult situation, showing respect can help your case. If you have to take a strong line there is a danger that it can be seen simply as an unreasonable attack; as such the automatic response is a rebuff. If the strong line comes from someone who is clearly expressing respect for others and their views, then it is more likely to be taken seriously, considered and perhaps agreed.

5. AIM HIGH

No apology for including some of the key techniques referred to before in this list (especially in Chapter 6 *The state of the art*). This is undoubtedly the most important. Indeed it conditions much about your whole approach. Aim high. Start by considering, in your planning, what this means. Think about what might be possible, think about what would really be best for you - and go for that. Remember that there is no doubt a list of variables - perhaps a long list - and that what you hope to agree is a mix of them all. Consider what is the best position in all areas - and go for that.

Negotiating is about to and fro argument, and about compromise, but it is very easy for compromise to become a foregone conclusion. You can always trade down from an initial stance, but it is very difficult to trade up. Once a meeting is under way and your starting point is on the table, you cannot offer another starting point.

Starting as you mean to go on is an inherent part of aiming high.

6. GET THEIR SHOPPING LIST

This rule links to the fact that you need to negotiate a package. If you agree parts of a deal individually, then you reduce your ability to vary the package because more and more of it is fixed. Something may seem straightforward in isolation. You are happy to agree it, yet suddenly you come to other points that you want to negotiate about, and there is nothing left with which to trade.

The principle here is simple. You need to find out the full list of what the other party needs to agree. Then you must not allow parts, possibly in fact important parts, to be picked off and secured one at a time, as a preliminary to hitting you with major demands at a stage where your options are limited.

7. KEEP SEARCHING FOR VARIABLES

Variables can be listed as part of your preparation; listed and prioritized. Even a thorough job at that stage can leave things out. *Everything* is negotiable, *everything* is potentially a variable – and this includes things that have specifically been excluded by one party or the other. You may have said something is unchangeable and then decide that you need the power that shifting a little would give you.

Certainly you need to question what the other party means. Does – *that's it, I definitely cannot go any further on this* – mean what it says, or only that they hope they will not need to negotiate further about something? Questions, or a challenge, may be necessary to find out. The search for possible variables and different mixes in their respective priority must continue throughout the whole process. As the process demands more compromise from someone then they may have to accept that things they had hoped could be regarded as fixed now have to be regarded as variables – and that some variables may need to be more variable than was the original intention.

Keep an open mind, keep searching and assume everything is always a potential variable.

8. UTILIZE THE TECHNIQUES

Your success in negotiations is less likely to come from some clever ploy or one display of power. It comes through the details. There is a good deal to keep in mind during a negotiation, and the situation becomes more complicated as negotiations proceed. You can influence matters in a hundred different ways, but they need to be appropriate ways.

The good negotiator deploys a range of techniques and so needs to be familiar with them and able to make the best use of them. But it is not a question of blasting the other party with a hail of techniques; they need using with surgical precision. Just when is it appropriate to be silent, or to show unequivocally that you are adamant?

Negotiating must never be allowed to take place on "automatic pilot" as it were. Every move must be considered, and this applies as much to *how* you do things as to *what* you do. Techniques must be made to work for you and the way to do this is on a case by case basis – one that reflects what is right for this person, this meeting and this moment of this meeting.

9. MANAGE AND CONTROL THE PROCESS

Certainly overall orchestration is a major overall key issue. It is all too easy to find that the concentration that is necessary to deal with the immediate situation, can result in your taking you eye off the ball in terms of the total game plan.

You need to take every possible action to help yourself stand back and work with the full picture. For example:

» make notes;
» summarize regularly to recap (and *always* if you feel yourself getting lost; you do not need to say why);
» keep as much of an eye on the broad picture as on the needs of the moment;
» keep your objectives and the desired outcome clearly in mind; and
» be prepared to take whatever action is necessary to keep on top of the situation (e.g. to pause and take stock) despite how you think it may look (in fact such action almost always simply increases the level of confidence you project).

If you approach this aspect of the process consciously, note what helps you, and allow positive habits to become established; then your experience and competence will build positively and quickly.

10. BE EVER ON YOUR GUARD

Never relax for a single second. Even when things are going well, when events seem to be following your plan accurately, when one agreement is following another – be wary. Do not your relax your attempts to read between the lines in such circumstances and do not assume that the positive path will continue. If you assume anything at all, assume that there is danger, reversal or surprise just round the corner and be ready for it.

Remember that *both* parties are doing their best to meet their own objectives and that the other person is just as likely to be playing a long game as to be a pushover. It is not over until it is over, and it is often late in the day that things come out of the woodwork and change what looked like, until that moment, a straightforward agreement.

Finally under this last heading, remember the words accredited to Lord Hore-Belisha: *"When a man tells me he is going to put all his cards on the table, I always look up his sleeve."* It is good advice. Similarly when contractual matters are involved – *"The big print giveth, and the fine print taketh away"* (J. Fulton Sheen).

As previously said, by focusing on the ten points above it is not intended to devalue any other point, and it should always be remembered that successful negotiating is a matter of getting many details right together. The first step to making it work is to understand the principles and something of the techniques and how to deploy them. With that in mind you need a conscious approach so that you make your experience build fast and note what works well for you to strengthen your negotiating ability in the future.

IN THE BEGINNING

In case you are left with any doubt that negotiating, and the details of it, matter, I will end with the story of the first negotiating in history (taken from *Hook your audience*, a sourcebook about using quips and quotes in presentations, published by Management Pocketbooks):

In the Garden of Eden Adam is comfortable, but lonely. He calls out to God telling him how he feels and God's voice replies from the heavens: *"I have the perfect solution, I can create woman for you."* Adam is pleased to hear there is a solution, but asks: *" What's a woman, Lord?"*

"Woman will be my greatest creation," says God, *"she will be intelligent, caring, sensitive, and her beauty will surpass anything on Earth. She will understand your every mood, care for you in every way, and she will make you happier than you can imagine. She will be the perfect partner for you. But there will be cost."*

"She certainly sounds wonderful" said Adam, *" – but what will the cost be exactly?"*

"Well" said God *"Let's say an arm, a leg and your right ear."*

Despite the promised return, Adam is not very happy about this. He ponders the arrangement for some time, finally saying, *"I think that's really too much to ask – what would I get for, say, just one rib?"*

And the rest, as they say, is history.

Frequently Asked questions (FAQs)

Q1: What is the relationship between selling and negotiating?

A: See Chapter 1 "What is Negotiating?."

Q2: What are the main techniques of negotiating?

A: See Chapter 6 "The State of the Art."

Q3: Is negotiating across cultural and national divides different?

A: Yes - see Chapter 5 "The Global Dimension."

Q4: What is the process of "trading concessions" and how does it work?

A: This is a core principle of the negotiating process - see Chapter 6 "The State of the Art."

Q5: What characteristics make a good negotiator?

A: This is one aspect of things investigated in Chapter 8 "Key Concepts and Thinkers."

Q6: How much of what is necessary to negotiate can be planned?

A: Planning and preparation are crucial – see particularly Chapters 4 "The E-Dimension" and 6 and 7.

Q7: There seems a lot involved in negotiating; how do I co-ordinate the overall process?

A: There is, and success is largely in the details – see particularly Chapters 6 and 7.

Q8: How can I fine tune my own negotiating technique?

A: See Chapter 7 "In Practice," especially the case setting out a discussion for analysis.

Q9: Where can I learn more?

A: Chapter 9 "Resources" sets out some of the options.

Q10: What are the key approaches involved in negotiating?

A: See Chapter 10 "Ten Steps to Making Negotiating Work" which pulls together the key issues.

Acknowledgments

I can claim no credit for the origination of the unique format of the series of which this work is part. So thanks are due to those at Capstone who did so, and for the opportunity they provided for me to play a small part in so significant and novel a publishing project.

My ability to comment on the issues here owes something to many people with whom I have worked in the past during my career in consultancy and training, and draws on the various courses I have conducted over the years. Until I set up my own operation in 1990, I worked with - latterly as a Divisional Director - the Marketing Improvements Group. Specifically thanks are due to that organization's founder Mike Wilson for encouraging me to write and for permission to encapsulate some of the company's corporate thinking about the techniques of negotiating into an earlier book. The conversation featured in Chapter 7, In Practice, is based on a role play session, which we set up and filmed to be shown at a conference; my thanks to my past colleagues Peter Kirkby and David Senton whose original thinking made this illustrate negotiating so well. They deserve much of the credit too for my getting into consultancy and training, staying in it and enjoying it so much.

A couple of the checklists used here are taken from my book *The Negotiator's Pocketbook* (Management Pocketbooks), as are some of the themes used in describing the negotiation process. I learned useful lesson about the contractual element of negotiating from my work with the UK Meetings Industry Association, which has members in the meetings and conference business, and this too is utilized here.

Last, but by no means least, thanks to Emily Smith who acted as researcher, searching out back-up material and references that saved me time and helped me meet a tight deadline. She took on the task at short notice and did a thoughtful, thorough and useful job; such help is much appreciated.

Patrick Forsyth
Touchstone Training & Consultancy
28 Saltcote Maltings
Maldon
Essex CM9 4QP
United Kingdom

Index